STRENGTH IN ADVERSITY

LESSONS FROM THE BOOK OF JOB

GARY NICOLOSI

STRENGTH IN ADVERSITY
LESSONS FROM THE BOOK OF JOB

Copyright © 2023 Gary Nicolosi.

All rights reserved. No part of this book may be used or reproduced by any means, graphic, electronic, or mechanical, including photocopying, recording, taping or by any information storage retrieval system without the written permission of the author except in the case of brief quotations embodied in critical articles and reviews.

New Revised Standard Version Bible, copyright © 1989, Division of Christian Education of the National Council of the Churches of Christ in the United States of America. Used by permission. All rights reserved.

iUniverse books may be ordered through booksellers or by contacting:

iUniverse
1663 Liberty Drive
Bloomington, IN 47403
www.iuniverse.com
844-349-9409

Because of the dynamic nature of the Internet, any web addresses or links contained in this book may have changed since publication and may no longer be valid. The views expressed in this work are solely those of the author and do not necessarily reflect the views of the publisher, and the publisher hereby disclaims any responsibility for them.

Any people depicted in stock imagery provided by Getty Images are models, and such images are being used for illustrative purposes only. Certain stock imagery © Getty Images.

Cover photo by Heather Bruce Nicolosi

ISBN: 978-1-6632-4849-7 (sc)
ISBN: 978-1-6632-4848-0 (e)

Library of Congress Control Number: 2023901110

Print information available on the last page.

iUniverse rev. date: 01/25/2023

STRENGTH IN ADVERSITY

LESSONS FROM THE BOOK OF JOB

GARY NICOLOSI

STRENGTH IN ADVERSITY
LESSONS FROM THE BOOK OF JOB

Copyright © 2023 Gary Nicolosi.

All rights reserved. No part of this book may be used or reproduced by any means, graphic, electronic, or mechanical, including photocopying, recording, taping or by any information storage retrieval system without the written permission of the author except in the case of brief quotations embodied in critical articles and reviews.

New Revised Standard Version Bible, copyright © 1989, Division of Christian Education of the National Council of the Churches of Christ in the United States of America. Used by permission. All rights reserved.

iUniverse books may be ordered through booksellers or by contacting:

iUniverse
1663 Liberty Drive
Bloomington, IN 47403
www.iuniverse.com
844-349-9409

Because of the dynamic nature of the Internet, any web addresses or links contained in this book may have changed since publication and may no longer be valid. The views expressed in this work are solely those of the author and do not necessarily reflect the views of the publisher, and the publisher hereby disclaims any responsibility for them.

Any people depicted in stock imagery provided by Getty Images are models, and such images are being used for illustrative purposes only. Certain stock imagery © Getty Images.

Cover photo by Heather Bruce Nicolosi

ISBN: 978-1-6632-4849-7 (sc)
ISBN: 978-1-6632-4848-0 (e)

Library of Congress Control Number: 2023901110

Print information available on the last page.

iUniverse rev. date: 01/25/2023

CONTENTS

Introduction ix

Lesson 1	When Adversity Comes Your Way 1
Lesson 2	When You Wish You Had Never Been Born 8
Lesson 3	When Your Life Falls Apart 15
Lesson 4	When There Is No Miracle 21
Lesson 5	When The End Is Near 28
Lesson 6	When You Hurt Too Much To Cry 36
Lesson 7	When You Feel Alone 42
Lesson 8	When No One Will Listen 48
Lesson 9	When Your Pain Won't Go Away 55
Lesson 10	When Your Suffering Is More Than You Can Bear 62
Lesson 11	When You Can't Challenge God 69
Lesson 12	When God Keeps Silent 76
Lesson 13	When Faith Is Vindicated 82

Pastoral Reflections 93
Endnotes 117
Further Reading 119
About the Author 123
Books by Gary Nicolosi 125

I DEDICATE THIS BOOK

To Bishop William Burrill
whose buoyancy, resilience and love of life has inspired me
and many others in the Church.

To the Rev. Dr. Keith Fleming, the Rev. Carolyn
Richardson, the Rev. Mary White,
Deacon William Zettinger, and Deacon Debra Loder,
all exceptionally gifted pastors and my colleagues in ministry.

In memory of the Rev. Brian McKay, the Rev.
Ned Kellogg and Deacon John Baldwin,
three of the most gracious, kind and faithful clergy
that I have been blessed to know.

To attorneys Gregory Thompson and Stephen Adams,
and my beloved wife Heather,
for their counsel, advice and edits of this book.

To all the dear ones in the churches in which I have served
who know the joy and pain of being human –
it has been a privilege to be your priest.

INTRODUCTION

No one is spared suffering. No one. This is a self-evident truth I have discovered in my many years as a priest.

Anyone who believes in God has asked the question, "If there is a loving and just God, then why is there so much suffering and evil in the world?" Human beings do horrible things to one another. As I pen these words, we are witnessing a devastating war in Ukraine, systematic persecution of the Uyghurs in China, deprivation of women's rights in Afghanistan and Iran, and North Korea's continued nuclear threat. In the United States there is rising crime, soaring gun violence, widespread homelessness, fentanyl and other deadly drugs killing thousands each year, millions of asylum seekers entering at the southern border, and billions of dollars in wire and securities fraud in the crypto currency market. Human beings can make a mess of the world, no doubt about it.

However, it isn't just social and moral evil – the abuse of human freedom – that causes suffering. Natural disasters such as earthquakes, hurricanes, tornadoes, floods, and fires result in the countless loss of lives. Add to this the pain that comes naturally from being human: rampant diseases, deadly viruses, and the inevitable decline and decay of our bodies.

Couldn't God have made a better world? The philosopher David Hume once mockingly suggested that God bungled the world rather badly.

Into this world of pain and suffering steps a literary masterpiece that has challenged serious thinkers and honest seekers for generations. The themes are as relevant today as when the book was written millennia ago: innocent suffering, persistent injustice, disinterested piety, religious disputes, and, overshadowing all else, the character and sovereignty of God.

It's called The Book of Job.

Job was a righteous man who believed God rewards goodness and punishes evil. Righteous people, he believed, are not supposed to suffer. And yet, he did suffer, and suffered horribly. He lost his health, wealth and even his children. This was incomprehensible to him. His belief that God caused his misfortune only intensified the pain. Job asked questions that we find ourselves asking when we suffer: What have I done to deserve this?

Why is God punishing me? How could a just God allow this to happen to me? This is not fair. Why, God, why?

When adversity comes our way, we, like Job, ask "Why?" It was asked by a man confined to a wheelchair after a head-on collision between his car and another driven by a drunk driver. Why?

It was asked by a woman who kept herself exceptionally fit and ran marathons until the day she suffered a stroke that changed her life forever. Why?

It was asked by neighbors of a Florida man sleeping in his house who was swallowed beneath the ground when a sinkhole opened right underneath his bed. Why?

It was asked by parents of a talented daughter with a promising career who was killed when she fell from a golf cart. Why?

It was asked by a student whose friend standing right next to him in the hallway was shot and killed in a school massacre. The student kept asking, "Why was my friend killed and not me?"

A prominent business leader suffered from Alzheimer's. He was reduced to complete immobility, strapped in a chair so he would not fall over. His wife visited him at the nursing home every day. She loved her husband dearly, but she also was exhausted by the strain of seeing him slip away. At one of my pastoral visits, she asked, "Why did God allow this to happen to him?"

I remember, too, a young teenage girl who collapsed on the school athletic field. She was rushed to the hospital where it was determined she would need a heart transplant. She waited patiently, prayed regularly (we all did!) and hoped against hope that she would receive her new heart. None came. Finally her body gave out and she died. Why did this teen's heart fail? Why did she not receive a new one?

I could go on… stories of tragedy and heartbreak abound – of young lives cut-short; of good people suffering more than anyone should have to bear; of loved ones dying all too unexpectedly. In one way or another, we all have been there.

Scholars, both Jewish and Christian, have tackled the theodicy issue: why a benevolent God allows injustice and suffering to occur. Frankly, none of the answers are entirely satisfactory. Most of us would struggle to agree with the seventeenth century philosopher Leibnitz who argued that

God created the best of all possible worlds. We are much more likely to agree with Voltaire who, after the devastating Lisbon earthquake on All Saints Day, 1755, wrote his comic satire *Candide*. Voltaire maintained this is not the best of all possible worlds but a place where terrible things happen to good people – not for any particular reason but because this is the way the world is. There is no making sense of it. All one can do is get on with life – tend your garden, as Candide does in the novel.

For the atheist, the problem of suffering is easily answerable. The world exists this way because there is no divine Creator who cares about it. There is no reason why things happen the way they do. Everything that happens is simply the way the world is. Natural disasters and human suffering require no explanation because the world operates without God and without purpose. This is the atheistic view.

If the atheistic view of the world is correct, then there is no need to grapple with the *why* question. Suffering and adversity happen because this is the way the world is. There is no pattern or meaning to any of it. It just is. All we can do is deal with it, try to minimize it if possible, and then get on with our lives.

The problem of suffering becomes more complex when you add God to the equation. Now the issue becomes: How can we believe in a loving and just God in a world of suffering and injustice? And what difference does our belief make? These questions pose a mystery. Reason can take us only so far, as the Book of Job powerfully shows.

An innocent man loses everything of value and demands to know from God why these bad things have happened to him. He has played by the rules. He has done everything right – worshiping and obeying God, leading a righteous life and being generous to the poor. And yet, God has treated him miserably, and Job demands to know why.

Job wants answers. He has been taught that a just God rewards goodness and punishes evil. That is what most of us instinctively believe, and it seems only fair. Most of the biblical authors in the Hebrew Scriptures embrace this view. It's an if-then proposition. If you obey God's law, then you will be blessed. If you disobey, then you will be cursed. The choice is ours: obey and prosper or disobey and suffer the consequences (Dt. 28-30; Ps. 1; Ps. 34:14-22; Prov. 8:32-36).

The difficulty for Job is that he is now confronted with an experience that conflicts with this dogma. His perception of the world is out of kilter with his beliefs. Does he change his beliefs in light of his experience or does he adhere to those beliefs despite his experience? Does he conform to the established dogma even when his experience tells him it is not true, or does he move to another way of thinking? This tension between dogma and experience makes for stimulating discussion between Job and his friends.

There are three debate cycles between Job and his friends, and additional comments by a young bystander named Elihu. By the end of the discussions, the reader is ready for some answers. Just what does God have to say for himself? How is God going to respond to Job's accusations? How can a just God allow for unjust suffering? The stage is dramatically set for God's answer. The curtain comes down and we wait anxiously for it to rise again for the final scene – God's answer to Job's questions.

How stunning it is, then, when God refuses to be put in the dock like an accused person and give an account of his ways. Rather than explain why Job suffered, or to give any justification for his actions, God reminds him of a hard fact: God is God and he is not. It is a stunning blow to Job and to us, the expectant readers of this story. When we demand answers, we get silence. When we demand to know why, we are told to trust. When we want to hold God accountable, God holds us accountable. When we think we know, God shows us that we know very little. In the end, as the prophet Isaiah puts it, God's ways are not our ways (Is. 55:8). That's it – end of discussion. God is sovereign and we are not.

Is that it then? Is that the take-away from this monumental work? There must be something more. And there is.

As we will see in our study, this book offers some of the most profound lessons that we, as God's children, can ever hope to learn – lessons about faith, the faithfulness of God and his goodness amid a lot of badness.

In the New Testament, we have a further revelation of suffering, especially with Christ on the cross. Here we discover a suffering God suffering for us, the innocent suffering for the guilty. The life, death and resurrection of Jesus provides us with an extraordinary understanding of suffering. We may never know why suffering comes our way, but God equips us with the resources to cope with it. Christians can even make the claim that suffering is redemptive. St. Paul wrote: "I am now rejoicing in my sufferings for your sake, and in my flesh I am completing what is lacking in Christ's afflictions for the sake of his body, that is, the church" (Col. 1:24). Our sufferings are mysteriously joined to the sufferings of Christ for the good of his people.

In the New Testament we learn that God's love conquers everything. One day, as the Book of Revelation tells us, God will make a new creation in which "death will be no more; mourning and crying and pain will be no more" (Rev. 21:4). For Christians, evil is seen in the light of Good Friday and Easter. Suffering never has the last word in our lives; God does. Where there is God, there is hope, even amidst the things we cannot understand and dare not accept.

What draws us to the Book of Job is our own familiarity with suffering. We have witnessed or, perhaps even experienced unbearable suffering. We know the pain of being human. Suffering is not a philosophical issue; it is personal – as personal as heartbreak, sorrow and disappointment. We have seen a world in disarray, the devastating effects of war and senseless violence, the destruction of the environment, and the pain and sorrow of so many afflicted by racism, bigotry, persecution, diseases and extreme poverty. Amid all this, we are encouraged to believe in a loving and just God who cares for his creation, strengthens us in our pain, and redeems us from sin and evil.

The Book of Job never shrinks from the reality of pain and suffering, and never stoops to simplistic answers in responding to profound questions. This is a book for people who know life is serious.

The thirteen lessons in *Strength in Adversity* can be used for individual or group study. Before discussing each lesson, I suggest participants read the lesson and the chapters of Job cited. There are discussion questions at the end of each lesson. However, I would encourage participants to ask their own questions and even share their experiences of suffering and adversity, if they feel comfortable doing so.

I have included a pastoral reflection at the end of the book which summarizes my own view of suffering based on the Book of Job but within the framework of Christian faith. I encourage those in group study to read the essay and discuss it after you have completed the thirteen lessons.

May you find in this study of Job a helpful resource to deal with whatever adversities come your way. Don't lose hope. Don't give in to despair. Don't quit on life. God is with you always and forever.

Prayer: Father, I abandon myself into your hands; do with me what you will. Whatever you may do, I thank you; I am ready for all, I accept all. Let only your will be done in me, and in all your creatures. I wish no more than this, O Lord. – St. Charles Eugene de Foucauld (1858 – 1916)

LESSON ONE

WHEN ADVERSITY COMES YOUR WAY
(JOB 1)

I had prostate surgery in mid-August, went back to work in late September, and felt amazingly well for the next several months. December, a demanding month for a priest, was predictably busy and filled with activities. Still, by the end of the Christmas services I felt great.

Then it happened. In early January I got terribly sick. Aches and pains, coughing, vomiting and fever. I thought all I needed was some rest at home, but my wife persuaded me to see the doctor. When I got to the physician's office, as I complained of chest and back pain, suddenly I became nauseous, sweaty and pale as a ghost. It was serious enough that the doctor called an ambulance to race me to the hospital. I thought I was going to die, but the medics were fantastic and knew exactly what to do to stabilize my condition. I sufficiently recovered in the next few days to go back to work, thinking the worst was over.

Since the doctors were not at all sure what had happened to me, I underwent a series of tests in the next several weeks. I went from one specialist to another, but finally got a diagnosis. Knowing I was a priest, the doctor looked at me rather sternly. "Father," he said, "you had a Jesus Moment. Consider yourself fortunate to be alive."

That diagnosis changed my life. I loved being a parish priest, but my life was in the balance. If I didn't change pace, I would be dead within a year. Still, I hesitated. There was so much work to be done in the parish. And yet the words of Charles De Gaulle came to mind: "The graveyards are filled with indispensable men." Finally, in April, one year after my diagnosis of prostate cancer, I announced to the parish that I would retire in August.

When adversity comes our way, our thoughts are flooded with questions. First, of course, is the question whether I will live or die? Is this it, the final chapter? When the prospects of immediate death begin to diminish, we turn to the practical: Will I be able to provide for my family?

Has the trajectory of my life made a permanent change – for the worst? Somewhere along the line, you may ask, as I did, the big question: "Why did God allow this to happen to me?"

This may be the oldest question in religion – reconciling the goodness of God with our suffering.

The Book of Job is the one book in the Bible that addresses the problem of suffering. It was most likely written at the time of the siege of Jerusalem by the Babylonians or in the post-exilic period of Israel's history – in the late sixth or fifth centuries before Christ. The prophet Ezekiel mentions Job at the time when Judah had become a vassal state of Babylon but before the nation's ultimate destruction and the mass exile of the population (Ez. 14:12-14, 19-20). After the conquest of the nation, only the poorest of the poor remained on the land. God's chosen people became the most wretched on the face of the earth. When a remnant returned to their land after years of exile, the people were poor, defenseless, and nostalgic for a world that was gone forever.

This is the context of the Book of Job. A wretched and humiliated people struggles to find meaning in their suffering. How could the promised covenant of God to his people be understood given the destruction of the nation, the exile to Babylon, and the present poverty and hardship? In answering this question, the Book of Job challenges the underlying theology in the Book of Deuteronomy – namely, that the just prosper and the wicked suffer punishment. The message throughout Deuteronomy is that if we obey God's law, we will be blessed. If we disobey, we will be cursed. Blessing or curse – the choice is ours.

Almost every good Jew believed this doctrine. However, after the fall of Israel, this doctrine begins to be questioned. After all, there were many good and faithful Jews who suffered at the hands of the pagan Babylonians. Was the nation so totally depraved that it had to be destroyed and everyone had to suffer? Couldn't God have used a less drastic means to spare the innocent? How could God be just and allow injustice to triumph? How could God be loving and allow his people to suffer so much? The Book of Job grapples with these questions that baffled the Jewish people – and still baffle us today.

Job's Piety (Chapter 1:1)

The story is set in the land of Uz – east of Canaan and on the border with Arabia. This is a land rich in farming with fertile ground and near a city for trade and commerce. Job has prospered in this region. He is a man of wealth, position and status, respected by his peers and loved by his family. He seems to lack for nothing. Moreover, he is a man of deep religious piety. At the outset, the writer makes clear that Job is blameless, upright, feared God, and spurned evil.

Job is **blameless.** This means he is spiritually mature, someone who possesses the attributes you expect of a godly person – living a devout, righteous and well-balanced life. Blameless does not mean perfect, but rather one whose heart is right with God. Job desires to do the right things, even if sometimes he falls short.

Moreover, Job is **upright.** He is straightforward and speaks the truth. He is a person of integrity. He is not duplicitous or dishonest. When he gives his word, he means it. In business and in personal relationships he is faithful and honest – someone you can count on to follow through with what he says.

Job **fears God.** He relates to God in awe and wonder. He has a deep reverence for God. He understands that God is God, and he is mortal. The German theologian Rudolf Otto described the idea of the holy as the *"mysterium tremendum,"* the mystery beyond human knowing that is experienced as awe and wonder. Job is an example of one who has this fear of God – not terror but adoration and devotion.

Lastly, Job **spurns evil.** This suggests that he keeps his distance from anyone or anything that might lead him into sin. Not only does Job not want to sin, but he avoids all occasions of sin. He never consciously puts himself in a situation where he might be morally compromised.

Job is a spiritually mature and straightforward human being. He reveres God and turns away from evil. We would expect God to bless him – and God does. Job has health, wealth and a loving family. He is admired and respected by everyone who knows him.

Gary Nicolosi

Job's Prosperity (Chapter 1:2 – 8)

Job is blessed with seven sons and three daughters. He seems to be an ideal father and family head. He loves his children and they love him. Here is a close, united family – no dysfunction or disputes.

As a father, Job takes exceptional care that his children remain right with God. He prays for his children, offers God sacrifices on their behalf and oversees their conduct and speech to ensure they do not go astray. Job wants his children to love God as much as he does.

Blessings abound in the life and household of Job. He is blessed with children (all ten of them!) and with great material possessions. He is a wealthy man with an abundance of land, animals and servants. Given his children and material possessions, Job has everything any human being could possibly want in his day. He is, without doubt, a blessed man.

Job's Problems (Chapter 1:9 – 19)

Now the scene shifts from Job to a heavenly council where Satan is a member in good standing. Satan means "adversary." This is where we get the term "Devil's Advocate" – someone who takes a contrary view from the accepted opinion to find fault with a person or idea. While God and the members of the heavenly council praise Job, Satan claims Job's conduct is basically self-serving activity done in order to obtain God's blessings (1: 9). Can loyalty and obedience to God be bought? Satan suggests so.

Satan's claim that Job has selfish motives in serving God goes to the heart of the religious life. Do we serve God to gain some benefit? Is our motive something other than devotion to God? In other words, do we expect to gain some value from our relationship with God? Perhaps we want a job, or good heath, or safety in our travels, protection for our children, or even eternal life in heaven. We pray and try to live a faithful life, expecting God to bless us. Satan argues that we are not serving God out of pure motives but out of self-interest. This is a natural spiritual struggle for anyone who believes in a sovereign and loving God.

Now, in the narrative, Satan plants the question: if the hedge of protection is removed from Job's life, will he still serve God or turn away?

Satan is getting at a fundamental issue in the religious life – not why people suffer but why people serve God. Do they do it out of self-serving motives or out of loyalty and devotion?

After obtaining God's permission, Satan attacks Job in a series of natural and human tragedies. His ten children are killed and he loses all his wealth and possessions. Job's world suddenly falls apart. He goes from being a man who had everything to a man who has nothing. Everything he valued in this world, especially his beloved children, are gone.

Job's Prayer (Chapter 1:20 – 22)

We might expect Job to curse God but, remarkably, he does not. In fact, he does just the opposite. After hearing the news of his losses, he worships God. He tears his clothes and shaves his head as symbols of his grief. He shows all the signs of sorrow we would expect of any human being after hearing such tragic news. Yet, he resolutely holds fast to his faith in God.

Grief and faith need not be in conflict in the religious life. One can grieve and still believe. Job models this tension for us.

There is nothing unfaithful about grieving our losses in life. Grief is a process God gives us to get through the emotional strain of loss. It is perfectly proper to cry because you miss a loved one who has died. Too often we try to minimize grief when we should allow for it. As the saying goes, "Don't take away my grief!"

One way to deal with grief is to rephrase a question we are likely to ask: "God, why did you take the one I love away from me?" Instead we might ask: "God, why did you let me have the one I love in the first place?" We can be bitter at God for the death of a loved one, or we can thank God that we had that person in our lives for the time we enjoyed together. When someone we love dies, we have a choice: bitterness or gratitude – bitterness over the death or gratitude over the life.

At the end of Chapter 1, Job expresses a poignant prayer that has resonated through the ages: "Naked I came from my mother's womb, and naked shall I return there; the Lord gave, and the Lord has taken away; blessed be the name of the Lord" (1:21).

Job was not praising God for what he lost. He was praising God for letting him have his children and possessions in the first place. His prayer is a lesson in stewardship because it reminds us that God owns everything and God can take everything away. Everything comes from God – even our fortune and family. We are not our own. We belong to God.

Routine problems and pains will always be part of our lives, but the real test of our faith is when severe suffering comes our way. Job refuses to curse God when misfortune happens to him. The chapter concludes: "In all this Job did not sin or charge God with wrong-doing" (1:22).

For Reflection

In his book *Good to Great*, Jim Collins wrote about the Stockdale Paradox. It is named after Admiral James Stockdale who was a POW for over six years during the Vietnam War. Stockdale was tortured relentlessly by his captors, but he managed to survive the ordeal.

Sadly, several of his fellow prisoners did not survive. These were the prisoners most optimistic about their liberation. They would give specific dates for their release, such as Christmas, Easter, or summer. These dates would come and go, and still they would be prisoners. The cycle repeated itself until finally they gave up and died.

Based on his experience as a POW, Stockdale taught us an important lesson. "You must never confuse faith that you will prevail in the end – which you can never afford to lose – with the discipline to confront the most brutal facts of your current reality, whatever they might be."[1]

Have faith but confront the brutal facts of your current reality. I saw this principle handled at the hospital bedside of a woman facing major surgery in the early morning. There was less than a fifty percent chance that she would survive the operation. I was there the night before the surgery to give her Holy Communion. After praying for her, I asked how she was coping. She said to me, "I don't know what it is, but I feel incredible peace right now. If I make it through this surgery, I'll be with my husband and daughters. If I don't, I'll be with God. Either way, it's going to be okay."

She did make it through the surgery, but only for a few days, and then she died. At her funeral there were tears for a woman who was dearly loved by her family and would be sorely missed. However, her family took comfort that she was not dead but alive in the Lord. While faith did not prevent her from dying, it allowed her to confront death courageously and confidently that the best was yet to come. Living or dying, she would be all right.

Questions

- Have you ever struggled with your motives for believing in and serving God? When we say, as Christians, that we are trusting God, are we saying that we are looking for a benefit from our relationship with God?

- From your perspective, is it really possible to experience both grief and gratitude when a loved one dies?

- What is the role of faith in coping with the death of someone you love?

Prayer: My God, I do not know what must come to me today. But I am certain that nothing can happen to me that you have not foreseen, decreed, and ordained from all eternity. That is sufficient for me. I adore your impenetrable and eternal designs, to which I submit with all my heart. I desire, I accept them all, and I unite my sacrifice to that of Jesus Christ, my divine Savior. I ask in his name and through his infinite merits, patience in my trials, and perfect and entire submission to all that comes to me by your good pleasure. – St. Joseph Pignatelli, S.J. (1737 – 1811)

LESSON TWO

WHEN YOU WISH YOU HAD NEVER BEEN BORN

(JOB 2 – 3)

John was a successful corporate executive. He had been with the company many years, worked hard and prospered. He and his wife were fortunate to live in a beautiful home in a gated golf-course community. Life was good.

Then John's wife Pat was diagnosed with malignant breast cancer. The news came as a shock to both of them, but their love supported one another throughout Pat's chemotherapy and radiation treatments. Although his work with the company was demanding, John tried to be with his wife as much as possible, especially during her chemotherapy treatments at the hospital.

There came a day when Pat was not feeling well and John was reluctant to leave her, but Pat insisted he go to the office for the board meeting. When he got to the office, the Chairman of the Board pulled him aside and asked, "How is Pat?"

"Not too well," John replied. "The chemotherapy has really weakened her."

"That's too bad," the Chairman replied. "I guess this isn't a good day for you. We're making changes around here, and you're no longer needed."

John could not believe what he was hearing. Not only was his wife battling for her life, but now this. When he left his home that morning, he wondered if things could get any worse. Now he knew. John found himself without a job, his wife battling cancer, and his company reneging on his contractual severance, including medical insurance.

In our last lesson we met Job. He was a man who had everything – health, wealth and children. He was a good man, but through a series of tragic events, he found that even he was not exempt from suffering. The remarkable thing about Job's loss of his wealth and children is that he remained faithful to God. Job's faithfulness was exemplary. He trusted God in the midst of that which he could not understand.

Job's Adversary (Chapter 2:1 – 5)

Satan had accused Job of a sunshine faith – blessing God because he had been blessed. Satan is proved wrong. Job continues to praise God in the midst of adversity and loss. Satan, however, presses his case in the heavenly council. He claims that Job only praises God because tragedy has not touched his person. "Skin for skin!" he says. "All that people have they will give to save their lives. But stretch out your hand now and touch his bone and his flesh, and he will curse you to your face" (2:4-5). Job still has his health and reputation, Satan argues. Even with his losses, Job could still start another family or even build a better business. However, if his health were taken away, he would have nothing. There would then be no benefit to Job remaining faithful to God.

At this point, we may wonder about the role of Satan in the heavenly council. In the Hebrew Scriptures, both in the Book of Job and in Zechariah 3:1-2, Satan is a member in good standing in the court of God whose role is to act as a prosecutor seeking to convict a person of their faults. He is always prepared to provide arguments to convict, even if the evidence falls short. No matter how exemplary the person, Satan will always seek to find some faults to charge against him. God apparently allows Satan to have this role, and even encourages him to make his case

Job's Affliction (Chapter 2:6 – 10)

God gives Satan permission to attack Job's health, but not to kill him (2:6). So, Satan afflicts Job with painful boils "from the sole of his foot to the crown of his head" (2:7). We cannot medically identify this disease, but boils imply some kind of inflammation. The boils covered his entire body, were visible to others and highly painful. Although not deadly, Job is afflicted with an unpleasant and even revulsive disease. The symptoms include itching (2:8); bad breath (19:17); loss of weight (19:20); insomnia (30:27); and darkening of the skin (30:30).

So serious is Job's condition, that his wife thinks it incurable and tells him to "curse God, and die" (2:9). Job responds by saying, "Shall we receive the good at the hand of God, and not receive the bad?" (2:10). Here he is giving the Hebrew view that both good and evil come from God – good by God's *active will* and evil by God's *permissive will*. God can permit evil things to happen for good ends. This is a difficult notion for us to accept. How could a loving and just God possibly permit or even allow evil, injustice and suffering to happen in our world, especially to those who are faithful to him? As we shall see, there is no clear answer to this question. In the end, we fall back on the belief that God's ways are not our ways.

Often, we want to know why we suffer, but God does not tell us. The reason is basic: God is not in the business of explaining himself. God is in the business of sustaining us. If we knew the reason, it would not take much faith to believe in God. Faith – the essence of real faith – is to believe in God without knowing why bad things happen to us. For us moderns, this is difficult because we crave an explanation for everything. Yet, faith is living with the mystery instead of demanding answers.

C. S. Lewis authored a popular book on suffering titled *The Problem of Pain*. Lewis wrote the book when he was teaching at Oxford University living a relatively comfortable and sheltered life. Pain was more a theoretical issue than one that touched him personally. The book makes several legitimate points, but it lacks the sensitivity and compassion for those experiencing suffering. One might even describe the book as Christianity combined with a British stiff-upper-lip mentality that bears and accepts pain as a way of growing stronger and better.

However, Lewis' reaction to pain changed radically when his beloved wife Joy – the one person who meant everything worthwhile to him on this earth – died. In *A Grief Observed*, published after his death, Lewis describes the symptoms of his grieving: anger, resentment, loneliness, fear, a persistent fluttering in the stomach and restlessness. How dull and flat the world seemed to him. He could find no joy in his work. Could God actually be, as Lewis lamented, a Cosmic Sadist?[1]

In the agony of his grief, Lewis tried to pray. Though his need was desperate, he sensed only the absence of God. He felt God had forsaken him. While he understood that all prayer is request, and that the nature of a request is that it may or may not be granted, Lewis wondered why God would not heed his plea. Pray he did, but there was only the locked door, the silence of God.

Lewis eventually realized that in his desperation, he wasn't knocking at the door; he was trying to kick it down. He wrote that his problem was one of expectation. He had a notion of what should happen, and when it didn't occur, he became bitter and angry. Our expectations should not be that God will get us out of adversity, but that God will see us through it. There is nothing in Scripture which promises that becoming a Christian means the end of suffering. Sometimes, in fact, it is just the opposite: once we become a Christian we experience suffering as we never knew before.

Think of St. Paul. He was a successful Pharisee, a pupil of the finest teacher in Israel, a rising star in Jewish circles. And yet, once he became a Christian, he became a targeted person. He received death threats, was stoned, whipped, jailed, and eventually executed (See 2 Cor. 6:3-10; 11:23-29). And yet, throughout his life, Paul never lost hope. Even as he awaited execution, he kept the faith and looked forward to an eternity with Jesus (2 Tim. 4:6-8).

Job's Friends (Chapter 2:11 – 13)

Job has three friends who, hearing of his predicament, immediately travel to him (2:11). Clearly, they care about Job and are willing to make the journey to visit him at his home. When they see his miserable condition, they do not speak for seven days, which is the customary time of mourning for the dead. Instead, they stay by his side in silence. This is their greatest gift to Job – their sympathetic and supportive presence.

Most of the time, the biggest mistake of well-meaning people is that they talk too much to a suffering person. Just being a sympathetic presence is sufficient pastoral support. When people are hurting, they don't need our philosophy or theology; they need our compassion. They want someone who accepts their pain. When ministering to a suffering person, we must never try to justify God or explain pain away. Instead, show compassion to the person and appreciate their hurt. Most hurting people do not want our answers; they want our presence. Give people love, not answers, and you will show that you are a true friend. Above all, never rob hurting persons of their feelings. Don't minimize how much they hurt, even if you think it is excessive. Never say you know the pain of another – you don't. At best, you can only seek to understand.

Job's Agony (Chapter 3:1 – 26)

After seven days, the silence is over. Job speaks, but instead of cursing God he curses his own birth. He regrets having been born, since he has come into a world where he has known such great suffering (3:3,11, 20-21).

In American law, many states have the tort doctrine of "wrongful life" which declares that non-life is preferable to a life of unbearable suffering and disability. Legal scholars, ethicists and moral theologians debate the validity of this doctrine that is designed to compensate parents who unknowingly bring a severely disabled child into the world. The argument is that it would have been better if the child had never been born than being born disabled.

"Why was I born?" is a question about my purpose and place in life. When our health fails and suffering comes, we ask why. Implicitly, we are asking for the purpose of our existence. Does my life have a meaning, even if I am disabled, handicapped, physically or mentally challenged? Am I here for a purpose or would it have been better had I never been born? What is the value of my life?

How poignant this is: Job expressed remorse over the very state of his existence.

Sometimes the problems of life can overwhelm us. We ask, "If God is in control of the world, then how could he allow me to suffer like this?" We cry out for answers, but none suffice. It even happens that our present pains cancel out the memories of past joys. When that happens, we feel overwhelmed by the darkness. That is the experience of Job as his friends come to be with him.

For Reflection

His health was failing. A stroke had weakened his left side and affected his memory. Soon he became incontinent and was unable to manage the workings of his own body. Then his emphysema worsened, and every breath became a tremendous effort.

I was his priest, and during times when he was in hospital and through therapy, I came to know him well. On one occasion he told me, "You know what the worse thing is about my condition? It's not the pain. It's not the therapy or treatments. It's not the incontinence or shortness of breath. It's the feeling of being so dependent! All my life I was in control and now I am in control of nothing!"

What do you do when life seems beyond control? No doubt we have all felt that way. You are seated in your car on the highway, waiting hours as the authorities deal with an accident blocking the road. You anxiously await an announcement from your employer on whether or not you will continue to have a job. The doctor tells you that your condition is incurable. There are so many things in life in which we don't seem to have any control.

And yet, we always have the ability to respond to whatever is happening in our lives. We cannot control every negative thing that happens to us, but we can control our response.

I learned this from my dear friend Robert Williamson. He was a Presbyterian minister who served a neighboring church across the road from my own. After an all too short retirement, Bob was diagnosed with terminal cancer. His world was falling apart, but Bob had this quiet trust in God which never wavered. When I last visited Bob at his home just weeks before his death, he told me how he was handling his cancer. He said, "I just prayed to God, 'God, here I am committed to you. I am here to do your will, in my living and in my dying.'"

Once the decision is made to hand everything over to God, the rest is secondary. Our world may seem out of control, but we are always under God's control.

Questions

- Have you ever been in a situation where you thought things couldn't get any worse, but they did? How did you handle it?

- Job condemns the day of his birth. He wishes he had never been born. What do to you think of the modern-day legal doctrine of wrongful life?

- Do you identify at all with the seriously ill parishioner who said, "All my life I was in control and now I am in control of nothing!"? Have you ever faced a situation where you had lost control over your own life? How did you handle it and what lessons did you learn?

Prayer: Lord Jesus Christ, by your patience in suffering you hallowed earthly pain and gave us the example of obedience to your Father's will: Be near me in my time of weakness and pain; sustain me by your grace, that my strength and courage may not fail; heal me according to your will; and help me always to believe that what happens to me here is of little account if you hold me in eternal life, my Lord and my God. – The Book of Common Prayer (The Episcopal Church, 1979)

LESSON 3

WHEN YOUR LIFE FALLS APART
(JOB 4 – 7)

She was an incredibly competent attorney, a senior member of the District Attorney's office in a prominent city. Defense lawyers dreaded facing her in court. She had a stellar record, winning almost all her jury trials. She was smart and savvy, and she knew it. She was an expert in her craft, highly respected by her peers, and considered one of the most powerful attorneys in the city.

Then, one morning, as she was drying herself after her shower, she noticed a lump on her breast. She dismissed it at first. She was too busy to get it checked right away. After all, it only had been a few months since her last mammogram.

A couple of weeks later, she had this hunch that she had better visit the doctor. The whirl of tests and appointments seemed endless. Within weeks she would be confronting not only her mortality but many other little deaths, taking an extended leave from her job, losing her hair, and then her breast.

It happened so suddenly. Within a matter of weeks this woman's life was turned upside-down. Today she is no longer a practicing attorney but an advocate for lawyer wellness, author and cancer survivor. However, constant monitoring of her body will always be part of her life.

Much the same thing happened to Job, only worse. He had lost his health, wealth and children. This once noble person had become a pathetic figure of a human being. He was relegated to living in dust and ashes, scratching himself with broken pottery to relieve his insatiable itch. More than physical discomfort, Job could not comprehend why he deserved to suffer so horrifically. At this point in his life he needs friends who will comfort him in his pain.

There comes a time when we all need friends. By friends I mean not just acquaintances or colleagues but people who listen and support us in our pain. Sometimes the most important gift we can give another person is what I call "a ministry of presence" – being with the person, showing that you care, offering a listening ear and a helping hand. Friends may not be able to heal the pain of others but they can comfort hurting people just by being with them.

Upon hearing the news of Job's situation, his three friends Eliphaz, Bildad and Zophar journey to be with him. They cared about their friend. They suffered with him. They sat with him in silence and listened to him share his pain. They were there with Job in his suffering, sitting silently, saying nothing, yet showing that they cared by their presence.

Then, after seven days the silence is broken. Job expressed his bitterness at being born. He asked why he did not die at birth, because it would have been better for him to die than to experience his present suffering (3:11).

To his friends, this was a shocking statement, since the Jewish people placed a premium on life. Yet, it is precisely in such times when hurting people say outrageous things that we need to be particularly sensitive to them. We must never ask or expect hurting people to deny or minimize their pain.

Every pastor knows that the ability to listen is a great gift to a suffering person. In fact, the greatest gift we can give a human being is to accept their pain – not explain it away, or minimize it, or rationalize it. Accepting the pain of another is part of a genuine ministry of presence.

At first, Job's friends sat in silence with him, but now they feel obligated to explain why he is suffering. They go from caring friends to amateur theologians, trying to reconcile the greatness of God with the judgment on sin.

Eliphaz's Rationalization (Chapters 4 – 5)

Eliphaz is the oldest of the three friends, and therefore by custom he gets to speak first. He asks Job not to get upset with what he is about to say, but feels obligated to speak the truth as he understands it (4:2).

Eliphaz makes a serious accusation against Job. He says to him, "See, you have instructed many, you have strengthened the weak hands. Your words have supported those who were stumbling, and you have made firm the feeble knees. But now it has come to you, and you are impatient;

it touches you, and you are dismayed" (4:3-5). In other words, Eliphaz is saying: Job, you don't practice what you preach! Eliphaz is disappointed with Job for not measuring up to the standards expected of him and that he himself practiced until his illness. He wants Job to reconsider his error by admitting that his sickness is the result of sin. If Job repents, God will restore him to health.

Eliphaz is expressing the dominant Jewish orthodoxy: that suffering is connected to sin. He tells Job that if he is living a good life, he has nothing to fear because God always blesses good people (4:7). He asks rhetorically if Job has ever seen an innocent person suffer to the point of death? Therefore, if Job is suffering, he is hiding sin in his life.

Eliphaz is telling Job that he cannot escape the consequences of his actions. Job is suffering because he sinned. In some way, he deserves to suffer because he has done something wrong. His wrongful actions have caught up with him. He is paying the price for his wrongdoing.

To prove his point, Eliphaz claims to have had a vision of God that made his hair stand up (4:15). In other words, Eliphaz claims some private revelation that sheds light on Job's situation. This is problematic from a theological point of view – someone claiming to have a private revelation from God that judges other people. The prophets in the Hebrews Scriptures had such revelations, but theirs was the exception, not the norm. Ordinarily, we should be leery of private revelations from people who claim visions from God, whether the claim comes from a friend, a pastor or anyone else. What they say may indeed be the truth, but the message needs to be discerned and evaluated very carefully. After all, If someone tells us what God's will is for us, we can rightly wonder why God can't tell us directly.

Special or private messages from God are always suspect and need to be tested for their validity. Even if we want some sensational message from heaven, God normally speaks to us through common events – other people, experiences, the church and the Bible.

Eliphaz goes on to offer a second argument, this one based on his own life experiences (5:1-7). Sorrow, he says, is part of God's plan for our lives because it sharpens and purifies us. Every disappointment or heartbreak can make us better and stronger. Our reaction to adversity is within our control. While we cannot control the tragedies that come our way, we can control our reaction to them. Human beings have the freedom to choose how we will respond to the life experiences that happen to us.

Eliphaz is on to something here. Yet, it is wrong when applied to Job. Even good theology may be wrongly applied. This is important to keep in mind because often well-meaning people will take valid principles from Scripture and apply them in a mistaken way. Applying the right principle to the appropriate situation takes discernment, and that involves analyzing a situation without bias or preconceived notions.

Finally, Eliphaz concludes that he believes all of Job's problems are the result of his sin. Job is suffering because he is sinful. In fact, even the suffering of the righteous has justification. For Eliphaz, God never afflicts suffering on someone without a purpose. So he tells Job not to despair of God's discipline but to accept it. "How happy is the one whom God reproves; therefore do not despise the discipline of the Almighty" (5:17). This view again suggests another dominant doctrine of the day – God disciplines us to purge away sin.

Job's Reply (Chapters 6:1 – 7:21)

Predictably, Job is not comforted by the words of Eliphaz. Indeed his suffering is intensified. He expresses the view that his very existence has become loathsome (6:4). He claims the right to cry out to God, because he is innocent of any grave sin. He is starving for understanding and kindness, not logic and lectures. He repeats his wish to die because his body can take only so much pain. This is not an intention to commit suicide, but he does ask God to take his life (6:8-13).

Job wants kindness from his friends (6:14). Here he is expressing a universal sentiment: what a hurting person needs most is kindness and compassion, not judgment and condemnation. After all, Job is living with a decrepit, failing body with worms and scabs, festering pus and broken skin (7:5) He is in anguish of spirit and bitterness of soul (7:11). He despises his life and can find no meaning in it (7:16). He awaits the day he will be no more (7:21). This is a man in deep darkness. The last thing he needs is a know-it-all friend who wants to tell him how wrong he is about his condition.

Job does not need sermons, lectures or admonitions from his friends. He needs kindness which is love in action. The Hebrew word *hesed* is best translated "loyal love" or "loving faithfulness" – a love that endures and persists through any and all circumstances. This is the love God has for us. In our human context, love tries to carry the burden of another person: to alleviate the load. We love others by our willingness to share the load with them.

In caring and supporting hurting people, we need to be mindful of two pastoral insights. First, physical and mental suffering cause people to say things they would never say under normal circumstances. Second, we must never minimize the pain of others. We don't know how other people feel when they go through adversity, because we don't have their background or experiences. The best we can say to a hurting person is, "I don't know how you feel but I know you must hurt and I am sorry." In other words, "It's okay to hurt."

For Reflection

Clayton Christensen was a much-beloved professor at the Harvard Business School before his death in January 2020. He also was one of the leading scholars in the world on organizational innovation and a hard-nosed numbers cruncher, deeply analytical and not someone we would consider introspective. And yet, in 2012, he wrote a best-selling book titled *How Will You Measure Your Life?* In an interview on measuring success, Christensen shared these reflections.

"Four years ago I had a heart attack. Then I was discovered to have advance cancer that put me into chemotherapy. About two years ago, I had a stroke. I had to learn how to speak again one word at a time.

"The more I focused on the problems of my life, the more miserable I was. And then somehow, I realized focusing on myself and my problems was not making me happier. I started to say, 'Every day of my life, I need to find somebody else who I could help to become a better person and a happier person.' Once I started to reorient my life in this direction, the happiness returned."

Professor Christensen concluded by saying, "The more important piece of planning is 'How are we still going to orient our lives on helping other people become better people?"[1]

In his book Professor Christensen said that many Harvard Business School graduates are successful professionally but deeply unhappy personally. At class reunions they admit not enjoying what they are doing for a living. There are numerous divorces and unhappy marriages. One classmate admitted he hadn't talked to his children in years. Another was on her third marriage. Oddly enough, their personal relationships began to deteriorate as their professional prospects blossomed.[2]

So, what was missing in their lives? It was a deep sense of meaning and purpose – to live for something greater than themselves, to make sense of their world, to know their reason for existence – that they are here on this earth not by random chance but by God's purpose.

Questions

- Can you think of a time of loss or suffering when you experienced the "ministry of presence"? Do you think a "ministry of presence" is an adequate pastoral response to someone who is suffering or should there be something more?

- How do you react when you hear that someone who is overweight develops heart disease, or someone who smokes is diagnosed with lung cancer, or someone who drinks heavily gets liver disease? Do you implicitly make the connection between sin and suffering, or that their behavior caused their condition? Are we naturally less likely to be sympathetic because of their conduct?

- Can you think of times in your life when someone has shared their pain or hurt? How have you responded to the person? Are there things you wish you could have said or done differently?

Prayer: Just for today, what does it matter, O Lord, if the future is dark? To pray now for tomorrow I am not able. Keep my heart only for today, grant me your light – just for today. – St. Teresa of Lisieux (1873 – 1897)

LESSON 4

WHEN THERE IS NO MIRACLE
(JOB 8 – 10)

One of the most poignant moments in my ministry came when a woman stood before a church group to share her story. Jane began, "Three years ago I went to the hospital for a series of tests and I was told that I had malignant cancer. I was also told that, although it was possible for me to take chemotherapy treatments, the chance of any remission was very slim. This was, of course, very bad news for me. I became depressed. I was ready to give up. All I could see was darkness.

"As I lay in this dark despair in my hospital bed, I started reading the Bible that was in my room. What I read there changed my life. It literally gave me a lift. I read how Jesus would go about the countryside and heal the sick. He would tell people, 'Don't be afraid; just believe' (Mt. 9:33). He even said that if 'you do not doubt in your heart, but believe,' you can move mountains" (Mk. 11:23-24).

Jane continued, "When I read these passages, it was as if God had suddenly brought light into my darkness. I came to understand that if only I had faith, if only I believed, if only I trusted God to heal my cancer, then I would be healed. Against the recommendation of my doctors, I took chemotherapy treatments. In the process I got very sick and came close to death. But as I stand before you today, my cancer is in total remission. I put my faith in the power of God to heal me and now I stand before you healed."

At this point in her talk, everyone in the room broke out into spontaneous applause. Everyone, that is, except for a quiet man sitting in the back row. After a moment he raised his hand and asked to speak. He said, "Your story sounds very similar in many ways to a story that was part of my life. It is very similar, but only up to a point. My wife also had cancer. She too believed in the power of God to heal her. She trusted God as the light to see her through the darkness. She took all kinds of treatments, and she too got very sick. Together we hoped, together we believed, together we prayed, and then she died." He continued, "Please don't get me wrong. I am very glad that you were healed. But as you stand here tonight, I have to ask you – why didn't God heal my wife?"

All eyes were upon Jane. The room was very quiet as everyone waited for her response. She also waited for her response, and then, discovering that she didn't have one, told the man that she was sorry for his loss and sat down.

How are we to make sense of this man's question? Jane was saying that we can make it through the worst of times if we just have faith. Isn't that how it works? Apparently, not for everyone, or at least not in the way we would expect.

Job trusted in God. He thought he was living a righteous and religious life. He was seemingly doing everything right, but then his life collapsed in one tragedy after another. His friends are no help to him. Eliphaz even intensified his suffering by claiming that Job's sinfulness caused his troubles. Now Job's friend Bildad speaks up.

Bildad's Accusations (Chapter 8)

Far from being kind to Job, Bildad begins by accusing him of being a windbag – literally someone who blows strong wind. He says, in effect, "Job, you are a cry baby and your complaining is a lot of hot air" (8:2). This is Bildad's response to Job's pain.

Bildad feels obliged to defend God. He reminds Job of God's character as absolutely just and fair (8:3). If Job is not guilty, then God would be unjust in afflicting him. That is impossible. So, Job's suffering must be deserved because it comes from a just God.

Obviously, Bildad's remarks do not comfort Job, but merely intensify his pain. Any time we feel the need to defend God, we will probably make a hurting person feel worse. Hurting people don't need to be pommeled into our way of thinking. They need to be loved.

Bildad takes his argument a step further by making a cruel accusation: Job's children died because they sinned against God. They deserved what they received because it came from a just God. Bildad must somehow make the case that Job's children deserved their fate. Their sin caused their deaths. While there are verses in the Hebrew Scriptures that seem to support Bildad's accusation (see Ex. 34: 6-7; Nb. 14:18), the charge does not apply to Job. There is nothing in Job's life that warrants such an accusation. Even if his children were not perfect, Job offered sacrifice for their sins, and there is no indication that God ever refused his offering.

Admittedly, there is a tension in the Hebrew Scriptures between vicarious liability and individual responsibility. Is our suffering the result of our own personal sin or the sin of others who are close to us? Different verses from different books can be cited to argue for different positions. In contrast to the verses in Exodus and Numbers, for example, the Books of Deuteronomy and Ezekiel teach that each of us is responsible for our own conduct and not for the conduct of others (Dt. 24:16; Ez. 3:16-21; 18).

Bildad believes that righteousness yields prosperity. This is precisely Satan's argument on why Job is not a true believer – he is righteous only because he is prosperous. Take away his prosperity and he will no longer have any incentive to be righteous.

Bildad takes an analogy from nature. He says that plants without water die. Since Job is withering spiritually, he must not be connected to God (8:11-13). Job, he says, is like a plant with shallow roots clinging to rocks. Such a plant will be pulled up and left to wither and die. God is uprooting Job like a bad plant.

We may raise our eyebrows in disapproval at Bildad's arguments, but the heart of his theology echoes other biblical passages. Bildad believes that God will not cast away the blameless nor uphold evildoers (8:20). This theology is expressed in Psalm 1. There the psalmist proclaims that the good flourish and prosper while the evil are chaff thrown into the fire. For Bildad, like the author of Psalm 1, prosperity is the result of living a righteous life. Suffering is the result of living an evil life. If we repent, God will take away our adversity (8:21). In Bildad's worldview, there is no room for mystery, nuance or ambiguity in the religious life. He refuses to acknowledge that there are some things in the religious life we cannot explain. Suffering is one of them.

Gary Nicolosi

Job's Answer (Chapters 9 – 10)

Job agrees that Bildad's theology is correct as far as it goes. It is not so much what he says as what he does not say that is at issue. Job is confused. He believes God is righteous and just even in the face of his undeserved suffering. Job is experiencing what psychologists term "cognitive dissonance." His beliefs are in conflict with his experience.

Cognitive dissonance begins with our adherence to an established or sacred doctrine which we believe to be true. However, over time our experience challenges and even conflicts with this doctrine. A tension arises between belief and experience. As the tension grows, the result is psychological trauma as we try to reconcile a doctrine that no longer resonates with us. We then begin to reject the doctrine as either untrue or only partially true. A "new truth" emerges that helps us reinterpret the doctrine in a way that is consistent with our experience.

Significantly, cognitive dissonance in the Book of Job does not just produce a disconnect between doctrine and experience, but a disconnect between God and our belief about God. Job believes God is just and loving, but he is now experiencing undeserved suffering. It appears God is unjust, but how does he dare argue with God about justice? Finite creatures are no match against an infinite God (9:3-4). Yet, Job wants to defend himself because his experience is out of kilter with his beliefs. He demands an advocate or an impartial judge to mediate his case against God (9:32-33).

A mediator works between two parties with a view of producing a negotiated settlement. Mediation is a way to secure something that cannot otherwise be obtained. Job cries out for a mediator so he can defend his innocence before God. He is convinced of his case because his experience of unjust suffering tells him he is right.

Job wants to challenge God on why he has allowed so much suffering in his life. And yet, Job knows he is a mere creature who dares not question the Creator. He has no right to a hearing and he believes God would not give him one (9:16). There is no chance that he could win his case against God, no matter how innocent he claims to be (9:19-20).

In Chapter 10, Job speaks to God and not his friends. He pleads with God: Do not condemn me, but tell me why these things are happening to me! (10:2). It is the lack of an answer to the *why* question that causes him so much agony beyond his physical and emotional suffering. He wants to know why terrible things are happening to him when he lived such a good life. It is undeserved suffering – a concept he cannot comprehend or justify.

The Austrian Jewish psychiatrist Viktor Frankl was arrested by the Nazis and sent to a concentration camp. Frankl's experience at Auschwitz forced him to confront the question of whether life was ultimately void of any meaning. At one point Frankl was forced to surrender his clothes and put on the worn-out rags of an inmate who had been sent to the gas chamber. He found in the pocket of his newly acquired coat a single page torn out of a Jewish prayer book which contained the primary Jewish prayer, *Shema Yisrael*: "Hear, O Israel! The Lord our God is one God. And you shall love the Lord your God with all your heart, and with all your soul, and with all your might."[1]

After the war, Frankl reflected on the time at Auschwitz in his book *Man's Search for Meaning*. He quoted with approval Nietzsche's words, "He who has a '*why*' to live for can bear with almost any '*how*.'"[2] Frankl discovered that human beings can cope with most any suffering if there is a meaning in one's life. In other words, if we live for something greater than ourselves, whether it be a cause or a person, there is a better chance we can survive even the worst conditions.

It is the lack of meaning, the lack of purpose, which drains the life out of us. That is Job's situation. His questions go unanswered. He lives in a world of mental chaos where there is no reason for his suffering. He cries out to God, "Why did you bring me forth from the womb? Would that I had died before any eye had seen me, and were as though I had not been, carried from the womb to the grave" (10:18-19).

Like Job, suffering may seem senseless when we experience it. In retrospect, if we can discern a purpose to suffering, we are more likely to endure it, even if we never fully understand it.

For Reflection

I began this lesson with the story of Jane who shared her miraculous recovery from cancer, which she attributed to the power of faith. However, at that same gathering a husband shared a very different story. His wife, too, had cancer, prayed for a miracle, believed she would be healed, but died just as the doctors had foretold. How do we make sense of two very different stories with completely different outcomes?

David Watson was a leading twentieth century British evangelist and priest of the Church of England. He had long been involved in the healing ministry and charismatic movement, but in April 1983, at the age of fifty, he was diagnosed with pancreatic cancer. He along with his family and friends prayed for a miracle. Prominent pastors flew from California to his home in London to pray and lay hands on him. English bishops and prominent clergy visited him, prayed for him, anointed him with oil and administered Holy Communion to him – all seemingly to no avail. Watson died on February 18, 1984.

And yet, in his death David Watson inspired us as much as in his life. He wrote a book published posthumously about his bout with cancer titled *Fear No Evil* which has helped people cope with their terminal illnesses. At the conclusion of the book, and shortly before his death, Watson wrote: "The most important lesson I have learned in these past eleven months is that God loves me, is always with me – in the dark as in the light – and that I cannot trust him too much. The best is yet to be, once we have put our lives in Christ."[3]

The cancer robbed David Watson of his stamina and vigor, but not his indominable spirit. He believed in a sovereign and loving God whose ways are not always our ways. We cannot predict, much less control, God's actions, but we can seek to be in God's will. As David Watson believed, even in the worst of circumstances, God's love is greater still.

Questions

- Philosophers would say that if God made a world without the possibility of suffering, there would be no freedom – freedom in the natural order and human freedom to choose and make decisions. Is this philosophical perspective helpful in understanding our own suffering or why God allows suffering to happen? How so?

- The circumstances of Viktor Frankl (imprisoned in a concentration camp for no other reason than that he was a Jew), is a stark example of unjust suffering. What do you make of Dr. Frankl's conclusion about the overriding importance of discovering meaning even amid suffering? Does that carry a lesson beyond dealing with suffering? How important is it for our well-being to find meaning and purpose in our lives?

- In what ways does Job's longing for a mediator between God and suffering humanity foreshadow St. Paul's declaration that "there is also one mediator between God and humankind, Christ Jesus himself human who gave himself a ransom for all" (1 Tim. 2:5-6)?

Prayer: O Lord, support us all the day long, until the shadows lengthen, and the evening comes, and the busy world is hushed, and the fever of life is over, and our work is done. Then in your mercy, grant us a safe lodging, and a holy rest, and peace at the last. – Cardinal John Henry Newman (1801 – 1890)

LESSON 5

WHEN THE END IS NEAR
(JOB 11 – 14)

Jack was unexpectedly diagnosed with lung cancer. He never smoked in his life, though he had worked as an executive in the steel mills in New York and Pennsylvania in the years before strict pollution and safety standards. The doctor told him that the cancer had spread throughout his body and there was nothing that could be done. Then the doctor said, "Go home and get your affairs in order."

How do you respond when you get a diagnosis of terminal cancer? Do you scratch your head and say, "But I don't deserve this!" We may know people in the best of health suddenly being told they have a terminal illness. Some people stoically accept the diagnosis and prepare to die. Others fight it even if that means experimental treatments that can savage the body. Still others travel to foreign countries and exhaust their financial resources in hope of a cure. Everyone reacts differently to news that they will die. Elizabeth Kubler-Ross and her colleagues listed five common responses: denial, anger, bargaining, depression and acceptance.[1] A common sentiment is that life is unfair.

Thus far in our study of the Book of Job, we have met two of Job's friends: Eliphaz and Bildad. When Job complained about his situation, claiming that God had unjustly punished him, Eliphaz responded by telling Job that he believed the right things but lived the wrong way. His belief was not coordinated with his behavior. Bildad gave an even stronger response, calling Job a windbag. God acts justly, Bildad maintained, therefore Job must take responsibility for his condition. For Job to say otherwise would be either to deny his sinfulness or the justice of God.

Zophar's Allegations (Chapters 11:1-20)

After listening to the blistering comments of Eliphaz and Bildad, Job's third friend, Zophar, speaks. He shows little compassion, and assumes Job's condition is due to his guilt. He accuses Job of babble (11:3). Zophar appears to be angry that Job maintains his innocence. This reflects his theology that mere mortals should not question or challenge the sovereignty of God.

Zophar asks Job, "Can you find out the things of God? Can you find out the limit of the Almighty? It is higher than heaven – what can you do? Deeper than Sheol – what can you know?" (11:7-8). God is beyond our comprehension. Who are human beings to question God's ways? God knows the hearts and minds of every creature, so who are we to challenge him?

Zophar waxes theological. He believes in God's omnipresence, omnipotence and omniscience. God is omnipresent or all-present, in and around and above all things. There is no place human beings can go without God being there. God also is omnipotent or all-powerful. There is not anything that God cannot do. Finally, God is omniscient or all-knowing. God knows everything even before it happens. Past, present and future are all one with God. There is nothing that happens without God knowing and willing it.

If God is all-present, all-powerful and all-knowing, then it is arrogant for Job to complain about his innocence. In Zophar's theology, all human beings can do is accept the judgment of God and repent of their sinfulness.

Zophar is an advocate of what we call today "prosperity theology" (11:13-20). He tells Job that if only he would repent, God would end his misery. His life would be better and brighter, and the dark trials over him would be over. The onus is on Job to repent and change his ways. Then God will heal him and restore his prosperity. Job should reconcile with God because it is in his self-interest. He will benefit from a right relationship with God. His troubles will be over. Repentance will lead to an end to Job's suffering and he will enjoy regained prosperity.

Prosperity theology is popular these days, and it is not difficult to understand its immense appeal. It is not that most people are interested in owning a mansion or a Lamborghini or even in becoming multi-millionaires.

Rather they tend to be people who have suffered bad breaks in their lives. They have struggled with finances or holding a job, felt inadequate and even desperate. Prosperity theology is their last resort – a hope against hope – that life will turn their way. It is like playing the lottery when you have only a few dollars left.

I am not disparaging people who are attracted to prosperity theology. My heart goes out to them. So many people today are surviving but not thriving, struggling to make ends meet financially, dealing with physical or mental health problems, coping with disabilities, or experiencing intense loneliness, low self-esteem, and failure in life. No wonder the message of prosperity theology is so attractive: get right and get rich. Get right with God and you will be tangibly blessed with material possessions and enjoy a happy, fulfilled life.

While there are verses in Scripture that seem to support prosperity theology, the New Testament is against it. After all, if prosperity theology were true, then Jesus should never have been crucified and the apostles should never have been martyred. The truth is that God never promised we would stroll through a rose garden, nor did God promise to tell us why we suffer. Right living and right believing do not mean an absence of suffering. In fact, they could mean just the opposite.

Jesus prayed intensely on the Mount of Olives:: "Father, if you are willing, remove this cup from me; and yet not my will but yours be done" (Lk. 22:42). Jesus did not want to die. If there was any other way to achieve his mission, he would have gladly accepted it. And yet, Jesus submits himself to his Father's will so that by his death life would come to us. He would eventually be resurrected and ascended into heaven, but as Martin Luther noted, "No cross, no crown."

When problems come our way, we are not without resources.

First, we have Jesus who suffered and died for us. We have a God who knows the pain of being human because he has been there. The crucifixion of Jesus is not a tale of God's indifference to human suffering, but of God's identification with that suffering. Only by undergoing suffering could God redeem it. The suffering of Jesus is redemptive because it is suffering love overcoming loveless suffering. St. Peter tells us that when we suffer, we are to look to Jesus: "For to this you have been called, because

Christ also suffered for you, leaving you an example, so that you should follow in his steps" (1 Pet. 2:21). By his suffering we have been healed (1 Pet. 2:24); by our suffering we may heal others.

Second, we have the assurance that God will be with us in our suffering. The last words of Jesus in Matthew's Gospel assure us that we are never alone but that he is with us always: "And remember, I am with you always, to the end of the age" (Mt. 28:20). Christ lives in us, and with us, in all the ups and downs of life. We never suffer alone. St. Paul, who suffered constantly as a Christian, wrote: "I have been crucified with Christ; and it is no longer I who live, but it is Christ who lives in me. And the life I now live in the flesh I live by faith in the Son of God, who loved me and gave himself for me" (Gal. 2:19-20).

Third, we have the promise that God will never allow our burdens to become heavier than we can bear. When we take up our cross, whatever it is, Christ takes hold of it with us. His strength and support is with us always. St. Paul who suffered some kind of physical infirmity (we don't know what it was), pleaded with God to remove it from him. Instead God replied, "My grace is sufficient for you, for power is made perfect in weakness." Paul concludes: "So I will boast all the more gladly of my weakness, so that the power of Christ may dwell in me" (2 Cor. 12:9). Paul lived with his infirmity for the rest of his life, but he continued to write, preach and visit churches until he was jailed and executed by the Romans. He is a model of how to deal with suffering in faith and not let it get the best of us.

And fourth, we can depend on God to do one of two things when life gets tough. God will either lighten our load or strengthen us so we can bear it. St. Paul says: "God is faithful, and he will not let you be tested beyond your strength, but with the testing he will also provide the way out so that you may be able to endure it" (1 Cor. 10:13). God's grace is sufficient for our every need, and if our burdens become too heavy, God will lighten the load or carry them with us.

In the face of adversity, we need to affirm two important truths: our confidence in God to deliver us, as well as our faithfulness to God even if we are not delivered. Remember, it takes more faith to suffer adversity than be delivered from it. So, here's the question: If God doesn't deliver us from suffering, will we still believe and remain faithful?

There is no better example in the Bible of faithfulness in the midst of suffering than in the Book of Habakkuk. A Hebrew prophet who witnessed his country invaded and demolished by the enemy, Habakkuk lamented, "I wait quietly for the day of calamity to come upon the people who attack us" (Hab. 3:16). And yet, after acknowledging the devastation of the nation, Habakkuk declares: "Though the fig tree does not blossom, and no fruit is one the vines; though the produce of the olive fails and the fields yield no food; though the flock is cut off from the fold and there is no herd in the stalls, yet will I rejoice in the Lord; I will exult in the God of my salvation" (Hab. 3:17-18). For Habakkuk, having faith does not mean getting our way. Sometimes life does not work out the way we want, but faith is trusting God, regardless of circumstances.

Job's Answer (Chapters 12:1 – 14:22)

Job's friends have offered shallow explanations of complex questions. In this case, the traditional teaching on suffering is inadequate. Their dogmatism actually distorts God's truth. The danger of all dogmatism is that it tends to misrepresent God (13:7-8) without considering circumstances and experiences that call into question accepted norms.

Job can't explain God, but neither can his friends. When we try to explain God, and categorize God into our way of thinking, we end up with something other than God. The truth is, we are not God, and therefore none of us should presume to know God's ways. We need to be humble, modest and reserved rather than give dogmatic explanations on why people suffer. Job, for example, maintains his innocence even as he is willing to face God's judgment (13:15). He exhibits a fierce resolve that his suffering is underserved while also acknowledging that he is a mortal and fallible creature in contrast to the eternal and infallible God.

Job compares his life to a flower that blooms, fades and dies (14:1-2), and addresses God regarding the fate of all human beings: "Since their days are determined, and the number of their months is known to you, and you have appointed the bounds they cannot pass, look away from them, and desist, that they may enjoy, like laborers, their days" (14:5-6). Job believes that God knows the month and day we are going to die. Whether we believe that, it is incontrovertible that everyone will die – it's just a matter of when. No matter if we are good or bad, faithful or unfaithful, we are going to die.

There was no clear doctrine of an afterlife at this time in Jewish history. Death was the end of life, as the psalms continually reiterate (See Psalms 39:5-6; 144:3-4; 146:3). Yet, Job hopes for some kind of vindication, if not in this life, then in another (14:12). He imagines death as either a sudden earthquake that shakes and disrupts a mountain, or as a stream of water wearing away the stone (14:18-19). Death may come suddenly or slowly, but death comes to everyone. The point is to use the time we have in this life to draw closer to God, examine our life, repent of any sin, and recommit to the God who saves us.

For Reflection

This lesson began with the story of Jack who was unexpectedly diagnosed with terminal lung cancer, though he never smoked in his life. Hearing the news of impending death, Jack could have become a bitter man. Instead, he managed to get into a conversation with a nurse which lasted several hours and covered many years of his life. Through it all, the word "hope" kept reappearing. After spending the night in the hospital, in the morning Jack thanked the nurse and said that he now knew what hope meant. He told her that he intended to go home and live his life as fully as possible, visiting family and friends, enjoying the Pennsylvania springtime, and finalizing bequests to his church and other charitable organizations. After leaving the hospital, Jack went home, had dinner and went to bed.

The next day I visited him at his apartment. He said to me, "Gary, for the last two months I have been unable to sleep well, but this past night I slept peacefully. I know the end is near, but I'm ready for whatever comes next." Jack had the kind of inner peace that we all should experience in times of adversity – an abiding hope in God in his living and in his dying.

In my funeral sermon for Jack, I referred to Thornton Wilder's *The Bridge of San Luis Rey*. The story takes place in a little village in South America. Each day the villagers make their way across a bridge to go to work in the fields. One day, without warning, the bridge snapped. Six persons fell to their deaths. There was a Franciscan friar that said, "Aha, I will do research into these people's lives and show why those six people were on the bridge when it fell. I will prove beyond a doubt that if you do bad things, bad things will happen to you, and if you do good things, good things will happen to you." The friar studied every aspect of their lives for six years, and in his book came to this conclusion: "Those six people were no worse or better than anyone in the village. God does allow the sun and the rain to fall upon the good and the bad."

The friar's book finds a place at a convent of nuns who care for the deaf, the mentally ill and the dying. The novel ends with the Abbess' observation, "There is a land of the living and a land of the dead and the bridge is love, the only survival, the only meaning."[2]

"Love, the only survival, the only meaning" – that is the only thing to say when an unexpected illness or accident comes our way. Through all the changes and chances of life, God is with us every step of the way. The ones we love die, but God's love never dies, not for our departed loved ones and not for us. Love leads to life – always!

Questions

- Do you think life is fair or unfair? Explain your answer.

- Do you believe God brings about suffering in our lives for some purpose or reason, or do you see suffering as a random part of life?

- Why do you think people are attracted to prosperity theology? Being honest with ourselves, even if we reject prosperity theology, don't we harbor (deep down!) an expectation that God will reward us for living a faithful life with health and success?

Prayer: If it so please my Maker, it is time for me to return to Him who created me and formed me out of nothing when I did not exist. I have lived a long time, and the righteous Judge has taken good care of me during my whole life. The time has come for my departure, and I long to die and be with Christ. My soul yearns to see Christ, my King, in all His glory. Glory be to the Father, and to the Son, and to the Holy Spirit. – The Venerable Bede (ca. 673 – 738)

LESSON 6

WHEN YOU HURT TOO MUCH TO CRY
(JOB 15 – 17)

During the pandemic, when many of us were stuck in our homes, I re-read a book I first came across in college, *The Plague* by Albert Camus. The 1947 novel describes an outbreak of a deadly pestilence in Algeria. Camus describes how the townspeople react to the growing threat.

Father Paneloux, a Jesuit priest and scholar, at first views the plague as a scourge sent by God on those who have hardened their hearts. As the plague spreads and affects a growing number of townspeople, Paneloux seems incapable of feeling their pain. Doctor Rieux, the town's doctor, says that Paneloux is a man of learning, but he does not seem interested in relieving human suffering, only using suffering to motivate people to draw close to God.

It is a fair point, one that Father Paneloux eventually comes to comprehend. He attends to the bedside of a young boy dying of the plague. He prays that the boy may be spared. After the boy dies, Paneloux tells the doctor that although the death of an innocent child in a world ruled by a loving God cannot be rationally explained, it should nonetheless be accepted.

That answer does not satisfy us – it certainly does not satisfy me. As the story unfolds, Camus's readers are more likely to take the side of the atheist Dr. Rieux who fights vigorously against the plague, doing what needs to be done without any fuss, even if he knows that the struggle against death is something he can never win.

The intellectual tension between Father Paneloux and Dr. Rieux exists today as we struggle with pandemics, war, violence, and tragedy. Is it God's will that human beings should suffer disease and senseless violence, or do we live in a world where the use and abuse of freedom in the moral order leads to dreadful things happening as a matter of course? Do we believe

Strength in Adversity

that nothing happens without God permitting or even willing it? Or do we believe that there is an element of freedom in the world – randomness or accident – and that tragic and terrible things just happen?

While the Book of Job does not argue for a random, accidental world, it does challenge the established doctrine that God blesses the righteous and curses the unrighteousness. We suffer because we sin; we prosper because we walk in the ways of the Lord. This theology saturates the Book of Deuteronomy and runs throughout other books of the Hebrew Scriptures. What makes the Book of Job important is that it challenges this theology.

Chapter 15 of the Book of Job begins with a second round of speeches, more heated and vitriolic than the first. What is at stake is not Job's suffering, but the doctrine of God. What kind of God would allow undeserved suffering? Or even worse, what kind of God would deliberately afflict one of his most faithful servants with unbearable pain? The very thought of such a God is too horrible to contemplate. Job's friends are afraid that if the righteous suffer, then there is no guarantee than suffering won't happen to them – or anyone for that matter.

Eliphaz's Reprimand (Chapter 15)

Eliphaz tries to shame Job into silence by accusing him of being filled with hot air (15:2). He goes on to say that "For your iniquity teaches your mouth, and you choose the tongue of the crafty. Your own mouth condemns you, and not I; your lips testify against you" (15:5-6). In other words, Job's own mouth condemns him, reflecting a corrupt heart.

Eliphaz is saying, in effect, that no one can dare challenge God. Job has only his own experience to fall back on, but tradition is on the side of Job's friends. So Eliphaz asks why Job doesn't accept the tradition, admit his error, repent and get right with God? According to Eliphaz, the reason Job is so stubborn is because he is a sinner who refuses to take the advice of his friends and accept the tradition.

Eliphaz has a point here. Job is one man challenging the established Jewish tradition. He is questioning the wisdom of the elders and insinuating that they were wrong for linking blessing with righteousness. One man against the tradition – how dare anyone stand against such venerable authority!

In Christian history there have been individuals who have gone against the tradition of the church. The Czech reformer Jan Hus was lured to the Council of Constance with a promise of safe conduct in 1415. When he got there, he was promptly burned at the stake as a heretic. The German reformer Martin Luther was more fortunate at the Diet of Worms in 1521. Thanks to the support of several German princes, his promise of safe conduct was honored, despite his refusal to acknowledge the claims of the Roman Catholic Church.

Job is like Luther challenging the tradition of the elders, and claiming that whatever the validity of the established doctrine, God does not always bless those who are righteous, nor does God always punish those who are sinful. There is a mystery to suffering that defies explanation. Job makes his case not on the basis of precedent or tradition but on his experience: he has been faithful to God but is afflicted with undeserved suffering.

In Judaism, tradition has enormous authority (15:17-20). It cannot be dismissed. A good Jew stands within the tradition, not outside it. To question the authority of tradition is to say that everyone before Job was wrong and only Job is right. Through this ongoing debate, the Book of Job grapples with the value and authority of tradition.

Eliphaz syllogistically summarizes the main argument against Job: 1) God punishes evil and rewards good. 2) Job is suffering. 3) Therefore, Job is evil (15:21-26). By implication, Eliphaz is making the case for his own righteousness: after all, he is not suffering. So Eliphaz is not only condemning Job as evil; he is defending himself as good. There is a danger here of rationalizing our theology to fit our experience. It's in our self-interest to affirm a theology of blessing when things are going our way, but what happens when life starts to fall apart? We must be careful about being judgmental towards others. That attitude leads to pride, which is the antithesis of an authentic religious spirit.

Eliphaz has a concern: If God does not always punish the wicked and bless the righteous, then why would people serve God? What is the motivation for being faithful to God if God does not bless you? This is an important question in the religious life, and one that Satan poses at the heavenly council at the beginning of the book. Is religion a matter of self-interest? After all, if we serve God only because of reward, aren't we operating from selfish motives? Perhaps so, since our motive is not devotion to God but our own well-being. The better response is to serve God because we love God, or even more, because God loves us. Thus, the question is reframed. Is the religious life a matter of self-interest or a matter of love? In times of adversity we are likely to discover our real motives for serving God.

The philosopher Bertrand Russell, who was an agnostic, claimed that he did his duty without any expectation of reward either in this life or any other. Russell's ethic is one that neither Job nor his friends accepted. They believed that God had to bless the righteous just as God had to punish evildoers. Reward and punishment in this life must be the basis of God's justice, or there is no justice at all.

Running through much of the Hebrew Scriptures is a reward/punishment ethic. Although logical, a reward/punishment ethic is a child's ethic. An adult ethic is based on love, loyalty, duty, and even sacrifice. The law is not to be understood as a bribe, and fear is not God's way to gain our faithfulness. As the people of Israel matured under the tutelage of their prophets, they came to understand law and morality as the basis of ethical living, not to avoid pain and suffering but to maintain faithfulness to the one, true God.

Job's Reply (Chapters 16 – 17)

Job begins his reply by expressing his disappointment at his friends for being such "miserable comforters" (16:2). He views his friends as shallow and incapable of appreciating his sense of injustice. Instead of empathizing with him, they condemn him. There is no attempt at meaningful conversation, only dogmatic pronouncements.

And yet, before we are too critical of Job's friends, we might ponder whether there is an Eliphaz in each of us. Don't we all quietly think that someone's adversity is the result of their own fault? We often fail to understand someone's pain before we respond to it. To show empathy is to be able to stand in the place of another and say, "I've been there" or at least, "I will try to understand." We need to avoid the tendency to judge people or theologize about their suffering. Instead, we should come to hurting people as listeners, consolers and encouragers.

Job, of course, is not perfect. His suffering has distorted his judgment. He levels at God a barrage of accusations: God has worn him out, left him desolate of all company, shriveled his body and shows him no mercy (16:6-14). Even as he cries out to God, he still feels alienated and rejected. Remarkably, he does not condemn or curse God. He simply wants to be vindicated before he dies (16:18-22). Given his awful physical state, Job believes he will soon die, but he wants to be proven right before his friends (17:1-2).

Job's friends think if they could persuade him to repent, his suffering would go away. However, if we are to minister pastorally to hurting people, we need to appreciate and understand their pain. Otherwise, our words will never resonate.

It is often the case that our own pain allows us to minister effectively to the pain of others. Drug and alcohol counselors, for example, are often themselves recovered addicts and alcoholics. They are able to minister effectively to others because they have been there. This is true for any of us who seek to help a hurting person. Those who are in the best position to respond to the suffering of others are those who have suffered. We may not have suffered in the same way, but we know the pain of being human and therefore we can relate to the pain of others. On the other hand, we will invariably feel inadequate if we seek to comfort others without first understanding their pain.

For Reflection

Margaret was quite frail and in ill health. Life had dealt her many blows. Her husband died in early middle age. She herself had battled cancer for over ten years. Her daughter's vision was deteriorating due to a rare disorder. Yet Margaret faced the world with a smile, a sense of humor and an outward calm that belied the difficulties of her life. She seemed to have within whatever life could dish out.

Margaret was a loyal choir member, attending church even when she felt ill, sharing with us her lovely voice and sparkling wit. She believed that it didn't make you feel any better to stay home, and that often you forgot for a time the discomfort of a failing body if you gathered with others. One day I commented on her buoyancy, and she replied, "Jesus keeps me singing."

Years after Margaret had passed away, I received a call that a parishioner, a severely disabled young woman confined to a wheelchair, had died after contracting pneumonia. The parents, Paul and Mary, were heartbroken at her death.

I was called to the hospital to be with the family and say the prayers at the time of death. When I concluded the prayers and gave the parents a blessing, Paul, with tears in his eyes, said to me, "She is now dancing with the angels in heaven."

Margaret, Paul, and Mary came from very different backgrounds, yet in the end, they placed themselves in the embrace of God. Their ability to face life and death is a witness that Christian faith is not mushy sentiment. It is a tough faith that allows us to face the future with hope and courage, believing that God is greater than our pain. For Paul and Mary, their daughter was now dancing with the angels in heaven. Or, as Margaret put it, "Jesus keeps me singing."

Questions

- Does having adversity mean one is bad? Does enjoying health and prosperity mean one is good?

- As you reflect on your commitment to God, why do you love God? Would you love God any less if you suffered misfortune, hardship or tragedy?

- Is it possible to effectively respond to the pain of others if we have never known pain or suffering ourselves?

Prayer: God our heavenly Father, in whom we live, and move, and have our being: Grant to this thy servant grace to desire only thy most holy will, that whether living or dying I may be thine, for his sake who loved us and gave himself for us, Jesus Christ our Lord. – The 1662 Book of Common Prayer, International Edition

LESSON 7

WHEN YOU FEEL ALONE
(JOB 18 – 19)

The 1976 film *The Front* is one of Woody Allen's finest movies. It is a dramatization of the Hollywood blacklist during the age of live television in the late 1940s and early 50s. A significant number of actors, writers and directors were labeled Communists or Communist sympathizers and as a result were rendered unemployable.

One of the characters in the movie is a comic by the name of Hecky Brown, played by Zero Mostel. The government makes life hell for him, affecting his ability to find work and pressuring potential employers to drop him from shows. Hecky finally gets an invitation to perform in the Catskills, a popular Jewish resort area in upstate New York. The audience loves him, but the club owner reneges on his promised salary, resulting in Hecky falling into severe depression.

Hecky realizes he will never again work in show business. His career is at a dead end. He can no longer support himself and the professional humiliation is agonizing. One night, Hecky checks into a posh New York hotel, orders a bottle of champagne; opens the window and jumps to his death.

Hecky Brown is much like Job – a person who has lost everything with nothing left to live for. Death is his only option. Unlike Hecky, Job will not take his life, but he too wishes he were dead, or even worse, he wonders why he was born. When suffering comes his way, he has to bear it alone, without any help from his wife or friends. He can't even go to God because he believes God has inflicted this suffering upon him without any justification. He finds himself isolated and in pain. His friends are no help to him at all.

In our last lesson, Eliphaz insisted that God punishes the wicked and rewards the righteous. Since Job was suffering misfortune, he had to be a wicked man and therefore was being justly punished. At the same time,

Strength in Adversity

since Eliphaz retained his health and wealth, he saw himself as righteous. He was blessed; Job was cursed.

Bildad's Denunciation of Job (Chapter 18)

Bildad now speaks again and he is incensed by Job's rejection of the counsel of his friends. He claims Job is out of his mind and has lost all sense (18:2). There is a law of retribution that orders the universe – we get what we deserve. If Job is suffering, it is because he deserves it. God is punishing Job in proportion to his offense. Job therefore should not condemn God but instead examine the causes for which he is being punished.

Bildad is well within the Jewish tradition in his argument. Jews believed in the law of retribution which is the rationale for the death penalty (Gen. 9:6) and is expanded in Exodus 21:23-25: "If any harm follows, then you shall give life for life, eye for eye, tooth for tooth, hand for hand, foot for foot, burn for burn, wound for wound, stripe for stripe."

Retribution is designed to make punishment proportionate to the crime, and it remains the basis for our modern-day criminal law. St. Paul in Galatians seems to accept retribution as God's order for the universe: "Do not be deceived; God is not mocked, for you reap whatever you sow" (Gal. 6:7). Even just people may suffer, but their suffering will be in proportion to their sin. The greater the sin, the greater the suffering. Sin has its consequences. This seems to be Paul's view based on the Hebrew Scriptures.

Keep in mind that both in the Hebrew Scriptures and the New Testament, all sin is deemed harmful not only to the person who sins but also to other people. Sin is both personal and social. It has consequences that affect others as well as us. In this life we reap what we sow, though not always perfectly. Injustice without punishment happens, yet Christians believe in a day of judgment when all people will give an account to God for their lives on earth. The Book of Revelation – the last book in the New Testament – is the Christian's assurance that God's justice and love will prevail.

Bildad's argument makes sense if there is only reward and punishment in this life. After all, how could there be ultimate justice if wicked people live prosperous and happy lives without any judgment or punishment in an afterlife? Similarly, if righteous people suffer for justice in this life, then what reward would they enjoy without an afterlife? If justice and injustice are confined to this life alone, the notion of a righteous God becomes more difficult to affirm. God must punish the wicked and reward the righteous in this life. The only alternative is an afterlife in which all human beings get their just desserts.

In summary, Bildad believes that every person suffers in proportion to his or her sin. Thus, all suffering is a manifestation of sin, and wealth and prosperity are manifestations of righteousness.

Job's Defense (Chapter 19)

In this chapter Job is both at his lowest and highest points emotionally and spiritually. He sees himself as tormented for no good reason. He feels there is no justice in the world. He believes that God's moral universe has broken down. "Even when I cry out, 'Violence!' I am not answered; I call aloud but there is no justice" (18:7). After all, how could God be just and allow such injustice to be afflicted upon him? How can he believe in a good God when he himself is experiencing such a bad life?

It is precisely when unexplained suffering comes into our lives that faith is crucial. Faith is trusting in God even when things go bad. No one can stay on the mountain top forever. Even the best of us will suffer, experience tragedy, and eventually die. Pope Leo the Great, in a sermon on the transfiguration of Christ, preached that although Christians should have no doubt about the promise of eternal blessedness, amid the trials of this life we are to seek for power to endure rather than for glory. Endurance in the midst of suffering is a hallmark virtue for a Christian.

In his own way, Job manifests endurance. He never curses God about his suffering but he does accuse God of injustice. He makes the accusation that God "has kindled his wrath against me and counts me as his adversary" (19:11). Job believes in a good God, but his experience challenges his belief. We can understand Job's pain. If we lost our health, wealth and children, would we not think that God had turned against us?

Strength in Adversity

Job's suffering is intensified by loneliness. Although his friends are present physically, they have abandoned him spiritually. There is a gap between them and him. He feels alienated from those around him (19:13-19).

Job then looks at his dramatic loss of weight and says, "My bones cling to my skin and to my flesh, and I have escaped by the skin of my teeth" (19:20). It may well be that his teeth had fallen out of his mouth, and that only his gums remained. Therefore, he must have had difficulty eating and having enough nourishment.

Job goes on to insist that his story be recorded in a book, since he believes that future generations will view him differently than his contemporaries (19:23-24). So certain is he of his innocence that he wants his claim to stand the test of time.

There is no doubt that adversity can cause us to question our faith. Pain can distort our thinking, make us say things we would not ordinarily express, and cause us to feel alienated from everyone around us, including God. However, in the midst of Job's dark night of the soul, he expresses one of the great statements of faith in the Bible: "For I know that my Redeemer lives, and that at the last he will stand upon the earth; and after my skin has been destroyed, then in my flesh I shall see God" (19:25-26).

Job believes that God's justice will prevail and that he will be vindicated, even if he is but dust and ashes. He is not expressing faith in an afterlife. Rather he is making a statement of confidence in his ultimate vindication by God, however that should occur. The remarkable thing is that Job makes this statement in the midst of severe depression.

Job's "redeemer" is more a legal advocate or defense lawyer who makes his case before the tribunal of God. Christians believe that Jesus is our defense attorney who makes our case before God based on his saving work on the cross. The notion of a redeemer runs throughout the Hebrew Scriptures and finds fulfillment in the New Testament with Jesus. A redeemer does for us what we cannot do for ourselves (see Lev. 25:25; Ex. 6:6; Ex. 15:13). Job believes he will be vindicated by God, though at this point God seems more like a prosecutor intent on convicting than exonerating him.

Notice that Job says, "*I know* that my redeemer lives..." This is not an expression of trust but of certainty. Job is basing his life on the certainty of

Gary Nicolosi

God's justice, even if he does not experience that justice in his life. While Job has no certainty of an afterlife in which he will be rewarded for his faithfulness, Christians believe the certainty of eternal life makes the pains of this life bearable (1 Cor. 15:54; 2 Tim. 1:12). We know that in this life there will be suffering for the best of us, yet we are not without hope (See 1 Pet. 1:3-7).

Like Job, we are all dying, even if we are now in excellent health. Our lives eventually end. Some of us may live longer than others, but we all die. We are closer to death today than we were yesterday. As the years go by, our eyes dim, our bodies age, our steps become slower, our muscles ache more, our endurance lessens, our mind is not as sharp, and we know that we are on the road to death. Our mortality should lead us to ask the question: "If mortals die, will they live again?" (14:14). Job does not answer that question but he believes he will be vindicated, whether alive or dead. Without any clear knowledge of an afterlife, Job holds to his faith in God's justice, even as he suffers without knowing the reason.

For Reflection

When I served a parish in San Diego County, my wife Heather and I would sometimes visit Coronado Island, one of the most beautiful places in California. While enjoying a cup of frozen yogurt by the bay, we sat next to a woman whose husband had died the year before. The couple had carefully planned their retirement, moved to Coronado, and expected to live long and happy lives there.

However, four years after moving to the island, her husband died. She was now alone and feeling terribly lonely. She was having health problems and was wondering whether she and her husband did the right thing moving so far away from their children who stilled lived in Chicago. "Well," I said to her, "at least you live in a beautiful community." She replied, "You know, when you are old and alone like me, it's not fun being here anymore."

Several years before meeting that woman in Coronado, I knew another woman in Lancaster County, Pennsylvania. Isabelle was an elderly woman living in a nursing home. Although she loved to read, she was near blind and suffered from a severe case of osteoporosis. Her children had sold her house, which meant that she would never return to the place where she had lived for over fifty years. It was an awful feeling, knowing that she would die in an institution rather than in the home she loved.

Isabelle was angry, and with good cause. She had lost her home. She had lost her health. She was nearly immobile and living in an institution where she was dependent on others for her daily care. She felt that God had abandoned her. "Where is God?" she would ask me. Then she would answer her own question. "God has turned his back on me."

Our conversations seemed to go in circles until one day I finally asked her, "Where is Jesus in all of this?" She put her hands on her chest, closed her eyes, and leaned her head back and sighed, "Oh, he's everywhere!" When I suggested that could be where she would find God, her eyes lit up. That was the hope she had been searching for – Jesus.

Shortly after our conversation, a pastoral visitor from my church became her friend, visited her regularly and gave her communion. When Isabelle died, the pastoral visitor was by her bedside praying for her.

Questions

- What do you think of the law of retribution: eye for eye, tooth for tooth, life for life? Should people get what they deserve, or does Christianity – Christ dying for sinners – change our understanding of justice?

- How does your belief in an afterlife affect your living in this life?

- What would morality and ethics look like if there was no afterlife? Would people act any different if there was no belief in heaven and hell?

Prayer: You were in me, Christ, you were always there, and I was not seeking you. When I had found you, so often I forgot you. But you continued to love me. From the depths of my being, a fire was rising to take hold of me. I was burning for you to be everything in my life. I was calling you: You, the Christ, are the only way; I have no other. – Brother Roger Schutz of Taizé (1915 – 2005)

LESSON 8

WHEN NO ONE WILL LISTEN
(JOB 20 – 21)

She lived on a beautiful estate surrounded by antiques dating back to the time of the American Revolution. Her friends were much like her, wealthy, sophisticated and from prominent backgrounds. They socialized together, enjoyed lunches at elegant restaurants, and went on cultural outings in the tri-state area.

One morning she called and asked if I would visit her as soon as possible. I was at her home within an hour. When I saw her face I could tell she was distressed. As soon as we sat down, she shared the news. She had been diagnosed with dementia, but it wasn't the dementia that bothered her. It was her friends. "You see," she said, "my friends don't suffer imperfection easily. You have to be perfect when you are with them. Dress appropriately, act appropriately, say the right things in the right way. If you show that you are imperfect, they won't accept you anymore." Then she said, "Gary, I am afraid they will disown me because I can no longer be perfect like them."

As it turned out, the woman's friends did not disown her, but she became more incapable of participating in the group. Wisely, she eventually moved into a continuing care community where she had social contact with other residents. Her once close friends would call occasionally but rarely visited. About four years after moving into her new community, she died.

What happened to that dear woman is not unusual in this day and age. There's a pernicious image some people develop of their community – whether a circle of friends or even a church. Their group becomes a kind of health club where members focus on keeping their bodies and minds in optimum condition. State-of-the-art exercise equipment, spas, expert trainers, a dietician and a stress reduction program are all available to members so that they can get into optimum shape. They worship at this image of excellence.

The problem in this club is that those who don't model its ideals find themselves removed from the rolls. Quickest to lose membership are those who are diagnosed with heart disease, cancer, dementia, or any untreatable condition. People who gain weight are likewise removed and their club keys are called in. In this health club, people are willing to be good to you only as long as you meet their expectations. After all, image is everything.

That is akin to where Job finds himself with his friends. They were indeed his friends so long as he met their expectations and measured up to their standards. However, once his life fell apart and he questioned the dominant religious dogma, his friends began to turn against him, not by leaving or disowning him, but by making clear that Job's views would not to be tolerated. Miserable though he was, his friends failed to empathize with his pain, nor were they prepared to listen to him in a way that showed genuine understanding.

Bildad's second speech was a merciless denunciation of Job, arguing that his suffering and misery is the result of his wickedness. Job responded by expressing his deep despondency over his condition. And yet, he gives one of the most powerful statements of faith in all Scripture: "For I know that my Redeemer lives, and that at the last he will stand upon the earth; and after my skin has been thus destroyed, then in my flesh I shall see God…" (19:25-26).

Zophar's Reprimand (Chapter 20)

In the face of Job's eloquently hopeful pronouncement, we might expect Job's friends to pause and even reconsider their criticism. Instead, Zophar begins his second speech by saying, "Pay attention! My thoughts urge me to answer, because of the agitation within me" (20:2). He is upset. Job continues to declare his innocence, despite all the obvious evidence that God is punishing him for his sinfulness. Zophar is indignant that Job would disregard the counsel of his friends and continue to claim he is innocent of wrongdoing.

Zophar appeals to history and the human condition to show that God has always punished the wicked and upheld the righteous. He contends that the prosperity of the wicked lasts but a brief time, but eventually they receive their just desserts (20:4-5). He then goes on to maintain that riches accumulated by the wicked are not retained, and they will be used to kill the sinner like the poison of asps (20:12-16).

Zophar is not entirely wrong. If you break God's law and engage in unhealthy or dangerous conduct, you may be susceptible to an early death or be punished by the criminal or civil law. Many dishonest and violent people are caught and punished, while others suffer financially or physically the consequences of their wrongful actions. There are, however, faithful and decent people who die prematurely of accident or illness. Others suffer needlessly or without cause, the victims of scams, frauds, libel, slander, and unlawful or immoral conduct. The truth is that the justice of God in the world is not easily manifest.

Zophar insists that God will cast disaster upon evil people (20:23). But is this truly the case? Isn't it our experience that there is not always a quick penalty for immoral or criminal conduct? In sixteenth century England, Richard Rich was appointed Attorney General of Wales after he perjured himself to convict Sir Thomas More of treason. As a result of Rich's untruthful testimony, More was found guilty and executed. Rich went on to reap his reward in Wales; he lived a comfortable life and died a rich man in his bed. So much for the justice of God – at least in this life.

Job's Rebuttal (Chapter 21)

Job counters Zophar's claim that the wicked die young. He asks, "Why do the wicked live on, reach old age, and grow mighty in power?" (21:7). He continues, "Their houses are safe from fear, and no rod of God is upon them" (21:9). Job claims that if you look at life objectively, the wicked don't always suffer. Indeed, he observes, some very wicked people live quite well. They seem to have fewer problems than the poor, and certainly greater possessions. Job layers it on: they may even have happier children and go to their graves without prolonged pain (21:10-16). So, Job concludes, in point of fact God's justice is not always meted out in this life (21:15).

Job then asks, "How often is the lamp of the wicked put out? How often does calamity come upon them? How often does God distribute pains in his anger?" (21:17). Job is saying that many wicked people live long, happy and prosperous lives. Clearly, God's ways are not our ways. We can't dictate to God how God must act in every circumstance (21:22-26).

Job challenges orthodox doctrine by citing his own experience. The two – traditional doctrine and personal experience – are not compatible (21:27-29). Experience shows that the wicked may be rich and powerful, while the righteous may be poor, helpless and suffering. Job's friends, however, remain blinded by doctrine and cannot see the reality before them. Dorothy Sayers cogently captured their mindset. "There is nothing you can't prove," she wrote, "if your outlook is sufficiently limited."

What Job wants from his friends is for them to listen to him, show more compassion, empathize with his pain, and at least appreciate his situation (21:2-3). Above all, Job wants to be listened to, without judgment.

Non-judgmental listening is one of the greatest gifts one human being can give to another, especially in times of adversity. You cannot be a good counselor without being a good listener. Hurting people don't want theological advice. They want a person who will listen to them.

Learning how to listen is difficult. The average person speaks 120 words per minute, but we think three or four times faster. It is hard to listen for any length of time because the mind moves faster than the mouth. While someone is still speaking, we have already formulated our response. And yet, listening requires that we discipline ourselves and refrain from speaking until the appropriate moment. Every effective pastor knows there is no healing without listening, no meaningful relationship without understanding, and no moving beyond pain without trust.

Here are seven practices for comforting a hurting person.

First, give the hurting person time to speak. Don't rush them or put words into their mouth. As a friend you earn the right to speak by listening.

Second, don't try to correct the hurting person. Let hurting people talk, even if what they say is offensive to you. Don't act surprised by what they say. Don't get angry at them. Don't try to explain their hurt away. It is far more important for a hurting person to speak than for you to give advice. They need to express their thoughts and feelings, including anger. The counselor's ability to listen aids in healing the hurting person because such people often feel lonely and isolated. By listening, you show you care.

Third, if you don't understand what the hurting person is saying, feel free to ask questions. Asking questions signals you want to understand the hurt of another. Try to ask open-ended questions that allow the hurting person to share about themselves. It lets the speaker know you are really engaged in the conversation and listening attentively.

Fourth, don't display disapproval or surprise at what a hurting person says. No matter how outrageous the speech, keep your composure. Arguing or correcting a hurting person is always counterproductive. Acknowledge the possibility of misunderstanding and a willingness to address it.

Fifth, don't be afraid of silence. Ten or fifteen seconds of silence can seem like an eternity, but sometimes a hurting person needs time to process what they want to say. Give hurting people the space to think through their thoughts before expressing them.

Sixth, look the speaker in the eye and show with your body that you care. Listening begins not with the ears but with the eyes. To be a good listener, your eyes should be focused on the person speaking. Eye contact is crucial to effective communication. In addition, listen with your head – lean forward, show interest, and use your entire body to listen. Body language is as important as verbal language. And remember: the least compassionate person is the one who does all the talking all the time.

Seventh, feel free to offer personal details about yourself so long as the conversation stays focused on the hurting person. Sometimes by sharing your pain you can better connect with the hurting person's pain. Whatever you say needs to be relevant to the hurting person. Be open, honest, concrete and conversational. Speak gently and sympathetically, offer non-judgmental love, and share yourself in a vulnerable but appropriate way that keeps the focus on the hurting person.

For Reflection

My church in Lancaster County, Pennsylvania hosted a pre-school for children with intellectual and physical disabilities. On a Monday morning one of the teachers came to school with a serious bruise that covered half her face, the result of her car swerving on ice and hitting a telephone pole. The teacher worried that her appearance might upset the children. One of the children, a bubbly and talkative little girl, when she saw the teacher's face, said, "You have a rainbow on your face." Where the teacher had seen the ugliness of bruises, the little girl had seen the beauty of a rainbow.

When we look at our lives, what do we see – the ugliness of bruises or the beauty of a rainbow? Maybe we need to rephrase the question: When Jesus looks at our lives, what does he see?

Perhaps a story about a little boy with Down syndrome will answer that question. In accord with the Roman Catholic tradition, this boy made his first communion at a beautiful liturgy. After the Mass, there was a family celebration. With the little boy standing nearby, an uncle said to his mother, "Wasn't it a beautiful liturgy? The only thing that's sad is that he understood nothing." The little boy looked at his mother's tears and said, "Don't worry Mummy. Jesus loves me as I am."

"Jesus loves me as I am." Are we able to say that? That we are all God's special people. That we are precious in God's sight. That our lives have value, dignity and worth. That as God's dear children, we are beautiful, loved and lovable.

Questions

- Do you have any experience with a social group, business or even a church that shoots its wounded?

- How can there be a God of justice if in this world bad things happen to good people and good things happen to bad people?

- What do you think about the seven practices to help hurting people? Can you share any other practices that you have found helpful?

Gary Nicolosi

Prayer: Let me hold fast to you, Lord, whom the angels themselves yearn to look upon. Wherever you go, I will follow you. If you pass through fire, I will not flinch; I fear no evil when you are with me. You carry my griefs, because you grieve for my sake. You pass through the narrow doorway from death to life, to make it wide enough for all to follow. Nothing can now ever separate me from your love. – St. Bernard of Clairvaux (1090 – 1153)

LESSON 9

WHEN YOUR PAIN WON'T GO AWAY
(JOB 22 – 24)

The week before my mother died, I was sitting with her on the couch discussing her finances. We had done this before, but this time she wanted to be sure I knew every detail about her estate.

The conversation was very matter of fact. Then, suddenly, it changed. We had just finished discussing her insurance policy when my mother fell silent. She lowered her head and sighed deeply. Then she looked at me and said, "I have been praying that God would lessen my pain, but it is getting worse. I have no strength left. Why doesn't God answer my prayer?"

Then she asked, "Gary, do you really think God cares about us?"

I will share my response in the reflection at the end of this lesson, but the question has been asked innumerable times by people who have suffered unbearable pain. When we pray for healing, do we really expect God to respond? Or, has God made the world in such a way that we are on our own without any divine intervention?

Job must have asked similar questions. It wasn't that he did not believe in God. He most certainly did. The issue for him was what kind of God existed – a God who hears and responds to the cries of those who suffer or a God who is content to leave us in misery?

Job is suffering. He needs friends who will listen and be attentive. Instead, he receives criticism, correction and condemnation. While Job claims to be blameless, he is not perfect. In his heart, however, he knows he is not the wicked person his friends believe him to be. His suffering is undeserved. Moreover, he cannot understand how a just God could possibly allow such unjust suffering to happen to him.

Gary Nicolosi

Eliphaz's Charges (Chapter 22)

Eliphaz now begins his third and final speech. He claims that God is too great to be benefited or disadvantaged by human actions. Therefore, it is only logical that God's judgments must be for the good of the individual (22:1-3). Sarcastically, Eliphaz asks, "Is it for your piety that he reproves you, and enters into judgment with you?" (22:4). In other words, "Are you trying to tell us that God is punishing you for being righteous? That is ridiculous!"

Given Job's miserable condition, Eliphaz can think of only two alternatives: either God is unjust or Job is unrighteous. This is the mindset of the dogmatist, the person who thinks in black and white and cannot appreciate nuance, ambiguity or the complexity of human experience. The dogmatist views life in dualistic terms: as either/or and never both/and. Beliefs are fixed, rigid and defined. There is no flexibility, no willingness to consider any new truths beyond established doctrines.

Eliphaz goes on to make three accusations against Job. First, he agrees with his friends that Job must be wicked or God would not punish him (22:5). Since Eliphaz cannot recite any sins of commission, he suggests that Job is guilty of sins of omission. Job has not given water to the weary and has withheld food from the needy (22:7). He also has sent widows away empty and children have suffered as a result of his callous indifference to the poor (22:9). However, these are accusations without evidence. Eliphaz gives no proof that Job actually committed any of these sins. In any case, disproving a negative is impossible.

Eliphaz makes a valid point but applies it wrongly to Job. Sins of omission are every bit as serious as sins of commission both in the Hebrew Scriptures and the New Testament. It is just as wrong not to do good as to commit evil. The Epistle of James says, "Anyone, then, who knows the right thing to do and fails to do it, commits sin" (Jas. 4:17). Jesus also focuses on omission. A vivid example is Matthew 25:31-46 in which the failure to respond with acts of compassion leads to judgment. *The Book of Common Prayer* has the penitent say: "We have left undone those things which we ought to have done, and we have done those things which we ought not to have done." Notice in this famous prayer that sins of omission precede sins of commission. In the religious life, not doing good is as serious as doing evil. Voltaire, who was not a religious person, put it succinctly: "Every man is guilty of all the good he did not do."

This presents a serious problem for one who claims to be blameless. How could anyone be justified if we are judged by what we failed to do but should have done? No wonder St. Paul writes that "all have sinned and fall short of the glory of God" (Rom. 3:23). How could we be justified if our sins of omission are held against us?

Second, Eliphaz accuses Job of thinking he can hide his sins from God (22:13-14). Then he warns Job that sinners are cut down before they can completely enjoy their prosperity (22:16). In the previous lesson, we have seen this argument rejected by Job based on his experience that there are bad people who seem to be prospering and enjoying life without any negative consequences. While Eliphaz bases his argument on dogma, Job rejects it based on his experience.

Third, Eliphaz calls on Job to change his way of thinking. (22:21-30). He tells Job to receive instruction from the Lord and lay his heart before God. This is good theology but the wrong application. Job had, in fact, laid his heart before God and sought his instructions. His problem was not his devotion but his condition. He could not fathom the disconnect between his loyalty to God and his treatment by God.

Job's Confusion (Chapters 23 – 24)

Job cries out, "Where is God now that I hurt?" The absence of God is the worst pain – the sense of God-forsakenness. "If I go forward, he is not there; or backward, I cannot perceive him; on the left he hides, and I cannot behold him; I turn to the right but I cannot see him" (23:8). Quite simply, Job cannot find God in his suffering.

Job wants to find God because he has questions to ask, and a defense of his life and character to present. He insists that he has not departed from God's commandments and that he treasures God's word more than food (23:12). His pain is not just physical but spiritual. He questions how a just God, a God to whom he has been faithful throughout his life, can thrust such evil upon him. It makes no sense to him, and part of his pain becomes living in an upside-down world where all standards of truth, justice and fairness no longer exist. He knows that no human being can confront God and win (23:13-17). And yet, he is confused about his pain and can find no meaning in it.

In Chapter 24 Job ponders the ways of God. Since God knows the future, why does he hide it from his creatures in the present? After all, if we knew the future, we could better prepare for it, and even withstand hardships in the present moment. Job then asks where is God when evil reigns? Where is God when the innocent suffer? Why doesn't God explain himself? (24:18-25). Job never gets an answer to these questions, either from his friends or from God. This is the issue of theodicy – of reconciling a loving God with a suffering world. As Job will discover, there are no adequate answers, or at least none that will satisfy the inquiring mind.

Suffering of some sort happens to every human being. The issue is not if or when it will happen to you, but how you handle it. Here are three practices to keep in mind when suffering comes your way.

First, don't play the blame game. Our temptation is to blame someone for our suffering. We feel somebody has to be responsible for our pain, so we begin to point fingers. Even Martha subtly blamed Jesus for her brother's death, when she said, "Lord, if you had been here, my brother would not have died" (Jn. 11:21). When we can't blame any human being, we blame God. Remember Adam after eating the forbidden fruit. When the Lord confronts him, he says, "The woman whom you gave to be with me, she gave me fruit from the tree, and I ate" (Gen. 3:12). In other words, "God, it's not my fault. It's yours because you gave me this woman!" Even insurance companies are notorious for blaming God for natural disasters. Companies usually have a clause in their policies referring to "acts of God" – as if God is responsible. Natural disasters, however, are not "acts of God" but the natural phenomena of a finite and fragile world.

Don't blame others, don't blame God, and finally, don't blame yourself. There are occasions when we are responsible for our problems. We need to evaluate our lives, acknowledge our sins and mistakes, correct course and move forward in the power of God's love. However, in many cases, the adversities that come our way are not our fault. When there is a car accident, the loss of a job, problems with our children, or health issues, we tend to blame ourselves. While we can always find some fault with ourselves, quite often there is really no one to blame, or the blame is on everyone, which means no one in particular.

Second, in time you will understand. Time is a marvelous revealer. It enables us to gain perspective on adversity. In fact, one day we will see our suffering from the perspective of eternity. Right now, we don't know the *why* of our suffering, but someday we will. St. Paul says, "For now we see in a mirror, dimly, but then we will see face to face. Now I know only in part; then I will know fully, even as I have been fully known" (1 Cor. 13:12). When the Duke of Wellington and his troops fought Napoleon and his army at the Battle of Waterloo in Belgium, just south of Brussels in 1815, news was transmitted by the use of lights across the English Channel to anxious residents in Britain. The words were spelled out, "Wellington defeated…" and a fog, so typical of England, fell over the channel. England thought the battle was lost and the dreadful news quickly spread throwing the nation into despair. But when the fog lifted, they could see the final word, "Wellington defeated Napoleon." The mood of Britain suddenly changed from one of tragedy to triumph. Think of our lives as living in a fog. We don't know the full story or the final outcome yet. Situations baffle us, events perplex us, and we cannot understand why things happen as they do. And yet, someday the fog will lift and we will see and understand. In the meanwhile we trust that God's love reigns supreme.

Third, claim the promises of God. When we rely on the promises of God, we discover the joy and peace God intends for us. When Jesus says, "In my Father's house are many dwelling places" and "I go and prepare a place for you," (Jn. 14:2-3), believe that when you die, you will be with him forever. When Jesus says, "I am with you always, to the end of the age," (Mt. 28:20), believe that Jesus is with you in all your doubts, difficulties and disappointments. When Jesus says, "Those who believe in me, even though they die, will live, and everyone who lives and believes in me will never die," (Jn. 11:25-26), believe that death is not the end of life; God is. When John's Gospel says, "But to all who received him, who believed in his name, he gave power to become children of God," (Jn. 1:12), believe that on the day of your baptism you were declared to be a child of God and an heir of eternal life. And when St. Paul says, "I can do all things through

[Christ] who strengthens me," (Phil. 4:13), know that you can rely on God even when your own strength fails you. In the end, God wins, and if we are in God, then so do we.

For Reflection

My mother sat on the couch waiting for my answer. She asked why God had not answered her prayer to ease her pain. I shared with her a story of my time as a newly-ordained priest on the Gaspe Coast of Quebec. I witnessed a good woman dying in great pain. Her death genuinely upset me, and so one day I went to Archdeacon Grover Kendrick, my supervisor, and told him about this woman's fight with cancer. And then I said, "The cancer won."

Archdeacon Kendrick, who was a wise and gentle man, got angry with me. "If the cancer won, where is it right now? Where is this victor?" he wanted to know.

"It killed her and it died too," I said.

"So the cancer is dead in the grave," said Archdeacon Kendrick.

"Yes," I said.

"And where is this woman right now" he asked, "if you believe what you say you believe?"

"She's with God," I said.

"So, who won?" he asked.

"God won," I said.

I got the point. God does care about us, in our living and in our dying. Our loved ones may slip away from our hands, but they never slip out of God's hands. For at the heart of the universe is the One who makes everything all right even when everything seems all wrong.

Archdeacon Kendrick taught me to be a pastor. On the Gaspe Coast I would minister to many seriously ill people, most of them were quite elderly. I would visit by their bedside, open the Prayer Book and recite the prayers for the sick. Honestly, though, I did not think my prayers were making any difference. Eventually, I began to doubt my ministry and I kept asking myself, "What good are my prayers?"

Strength in Adversity

Again, I went to Archdeacon Kendrick. I told him my doubts about praying for the sick. "Gary," he said, "it is not for you to play God and decide who should get well and who should die. Your job is to be Christ's representative to these people. You are to show them love, kindness, compassion, and to pray for them when they are sick or in trouble. You pray for their healing, but then you let God act in each person as God chooses." He ended with words I will never forget: "Don't bring God down to your size. Let God be God."

Questions

- Do you think it is possible for someone to experience God's presence when they are in pain? If so, how?

- What do you think of the distinction between sins of omission and commission? Given that distinction, can anyone claim to be blameless?

- What do you think of the three practices for coping with suffering? Do they ring true in your life? What other practices help you?

Prayer: Thanks be to you, Lord Jesus Christ, for all the benefits which you have won for us, for all the pains and insults which you have borne for us. O most merciful Redeemer, Friend and Brother, may we know you more clearly, love you more dearly, and follow you more nearly, day by day. – St. Richard of Chichester (1198 – 1253)

LESSON 10

WHEN YOUR SUFFERING IS MORE THAN YOU CAN BEAR
(JOB 25 – 31)

We know the name Billy Graham. He was the most prominent evangelist of the twentieth century who preached to millions of people around the world. When Billy Graham began his ministry back in the 1940s, there was another evangelist, a Canadian, who was equally passionate about preaching the Gospel and converting souls. His name was Charles Templeton. However, along the way, Templeton abandoned his ministry and became an agnostic. In his book *Farewell to God*, Templeton recounted his journey from belief to unbelief. He claimed that he always had doubts about Christianity, but one thing put him over the edge. It was a picture in *Life* magazine of a poor African woman holding her dead baby in her arms. The child had starved to death during a long draught in Northern Africa. The moment he saw the picture, Charles Templeton gave up his belief in God.

Who among us has not had such doubts, especially when tragedy hits close to home? And yet, faith is a matter of living with our doubts and uncertainties, and still saying, "I believe."

No one reflects this view better than the vicar in Margaret Craven's novel *I Heard the Owl Call My Name*. The story is about a young priest assigned to a remote First Nations village in northern British Columbia. One day the priest encounters a disgruntled teacher who is utterly dissatisfied with the primitive living conditions in the village. The teacher tells the priest that he is an atheist. Christianity, he says, is a calamity. Anyone who professes it must be incredibly naïve.

The story continues: "The young vicar grinned and agreed. There were two kinds of naivete, he said, quoting Schweitzer. One not even aware of the problems, and another which has knocked on all the doors of knowledge and knows man can explain little and still is willing to follow his convictions into the unknown. 'This takes courage' he said, and he thanked the teacher and returned to the vicarage."[1]

Unlike the preacher-turned-agnostic Charles Templeton, Job is not observing the suffering of others; he is experiencing it himself. His pain is his own. And yet, like the vicar in Margaret Craven's novel, Job refuses to walk away from God, despite his doubts and uncertainties. He wonders aloud why a loving and just God would cause him such undeserved suffering. When tragedy came upon him, and he lost everything of value, he asked the question we would ask: "Why did God do this to me?" It is this *why* question that intensifies Job's suffering beyond his physical pain and the loss of his wealth and children. By their belligerence, Job's friends only make his pain worse.

Bildad's Last Argument (Chapter 25)

Bildad gives the last and shortest speech from Job's friends. He repeats themes already stressed: the greatness of God and the insignificance of human beings. Bildad goes so far as to say that in contrast to God, a human being is a mere "worm" (25:6).

Bildad's point is well taken. God is far greater than our understanding. There is no infallible way of knowing God's ways. Such advice should have been heeded by Bildad and his friends. Rather than living with the mystery of God, they sought to define God's ways according to their own understanding. Unintentionally, they brought God down to their own size. This is always the danger of anyone who claims to know God's ways with certainty. Humility is a prerequisite to discerning God's will and ways. There is an immense gap between the Creator and the creature which is bridged by God's revelation in Scripture and the Holy Spirit. Supreme Court Justice Oliver Wendell Holmes, in a letter to philosopher William James, wrote: "The great act of faith is when a man decides he is not God." Holmes, who was a Unitarian, recognized both the mystery of God and the fallibility of human beings.

Job's Description of God's Majesty (Chapters 26 – 28)

Job rebukes his friends for failing to console him (26:1-4) and offers an eloquent soliloquy on God's majesty and power. We are not to understand Job's words scientifically but poetically. Within his own limited frame of knowledge, he is attempting to describe the glory and wonder of God. Job deeply respects God's mystery and majesty. He never ceases to be in awe of God's sovereignty even when he cannot understand or much less accept God's ways.

Job then reaffirms his innocence (27:1-6). He tells his friends that God doesn't always work in a predictable way. No one can presume to know God's ways with certainty. There is always a mystery to God beyond our understanding. While affirming that God does indeed punish the unjust, Job insists mere mortals cannot always see God's ways (27:8-23).

So, where does wisdom lie? "Truly," Job declares," the fear of the Lord, that is wisdom; and to depart from evil is understanding" (28:28). Fear of the Lord is not terror but loving awe. It does not paralyze but energize. It is reverence for God who is the mystery beyond human comprehension. In the face of God's majesty, it is pride to demand answers from God when things don't go our way. We have no right to demand anything from God. The only way to approach God is with humility.

Job's Desire for the Past (Chapters 29 – 31)

What follows is heart wrenching. Job longs for the days when life was good (29:2). He gives a nostalgic account of days gone by when he had prosperity, health and children. He yearns for the days when he was respected by his peers. People in the city would comment on how much he helped the poor and orphans (29:12), and those who were victims of wicked people (29:17).

While there is a natural tendency for anyone suffering in the present to look back nostalgically to the past, in Job's case the past was indeed better than the present. The "good old days" were, in fact, good. Job had what any human being in his day could possibly want: a devoted family, business success, good health and a stellar reputation. We can empathize with Job for looking back through gauzy memory. Life took a bad turn for him and the past was better.

When things take a turn for the worse, we, like Job, are tempted to nostalgia – to look back on the past as a golden age. We look back with joy and look to our present circumstances with sorrow. The past seems to have had less stress, fewer responsibilities and smaller problems than the present, but, for most of us, this is a delusion caused by our suffering. The tendency is to idealize the past by making it better than it actually was. If we are honest, the past was not as good as we think.

The truth is, we had problems in the good old days. Heartaches and heartbreaks are in every time and place. No time is problem free. Suffering causes us to have a selective memory – to focus on the things that were pleasant and to block from our minds the things that were difficult.

The mistake many of us make is to think that we can live a life devoid of suffering. This is impossible. There is no problem-free living. Each stage of life has its own challenges. The high school student dealing with puberty struggles as much as the middle-aged worker who is unhappy with his or her job or the retiree coping with health issues. We all face difficulties throughout every stage of life. It is wise advice not to make the present seem worse than it is by comparing it with a past censored of suffering and adversity.

Job's wistful look back only intensifies his present day pain and humiliation. He contrasts the respect he enjoyed in former days with his disgrace in the present. Even young men, who are supposed to show respect to their elders, now mock him (30:1). What makes the humiliation even more difficult to bear is that the fathers of the mockers are from a lower social class that used to defer to him. In a world of hierarchy and class structure, that kind of humiliation was deeply distressful to Job. His pain is sheer agony (30:7) and again he wonders why God has smitten him (30:20-22). His only comfort is the music of the harp which soothes his soul (30:31).

Job turns to the question of particularized wrong-doing. He denies sexual sin or deceitful business practices. He claims his personal and professional lives are exemplary (31:1-15). From his vantage point, he passes the character test: What he does in private is what he wants known in public. His public and private lives are in sync.

Remarkably, Job denies any hatred or bitterness toward his enemies. At a time when vengeance against injury was common, Job denies being guilty of any violent or retaliatory conduct against others (31:16-23). Here is a man seeking to follow the law laid down in Leviticus: "You shall not take vengeance or bear a grudge against any of your people, but you shall love your neighbor as yourself" (Lev. 19:18).

After defending himself against these particular and familiar sins, Job is done. He rests his case: "Oh, that I had one to hear me!" he laments. "Let the Almighty answer me! (31:35). He prays once more for an answer from God on why he has been so afflicted. Yet, at this point God remains silent. Having made his case, Job can say no more.

God's Purpose for Suffering

The Book of Job does not give us a definitive answer on why a loving God allows so much suffering, especially of the innocent. For that we must look to the New Testament.

Romans 8:28 is a key verse in understanding the ways of God. St. Paul writes: "We know that all things work together for good for those who love God, who are called according to his purpose." It is important to note what this verse does not say. It doesn't say God causes everything that happens to us. Nor does it say that everything that happens to us is good. And it does not say that everything that happens to us is going to turn out good for everybody involved. What it does say is that God can cause good to come out of all things. The phrase "all things" is inclusive – it means our entire life experience from birth to death.

However, St. Paul is not through. Romans 8:28 must be read in conjunction with Romans 8:29: "For those whom he foreknew he also predestined to be conformed to the image of his Son, in order that he might be the firstborn within a large family." God can take the bad things that happen to us and use them for good. God has a purpose for human beings – that we are conformed to the image of his Son. To make us like Jesus, God uses some distasteful experiences in life. God takes what is bad, puts it into the right context, and makes us better. So, everything that happens to us – no matter how bad – can make us better. Like it or not, God is much more interested in our character than our comfort.

St. Paul says that "all things work together for good" – not for our joy. Many things happen to us that do not bring us joy. That is not their purpose. We are here on this earth to give honor and glory to God through a holy life. Everything else is secondary.

For Reflection

Mary was a successful CPA in her early fifties and she was going blind. She went from doctor to doctor and they put her on special diets and gave her special treatments, but nothing seemed to stop the steady loss of her vision. Finally, an eye specialist told Mary she had one last option. There was a very complicated surgery that could be performed. If it were successful, she would be able to save some of her vison. If unsuccessful, she would go completely blind. Mary chose to have the surgery. She emerged from that operation with no sight at all and no hope for that ever to change.

When I visited Mary in the hospital, she said, "During these last months I have often thought of myself as a candle about to go out. I thought that everything I am, is tied up in being able to see. I expected that when blackness came, then there would be nothingness. Now I'm blind. It's dark. But I'm still here. I'm still me. God is still God. It's going to be okay, somehow."

We all have our own terrible times. Some of us may suffer more than others, but we all have our dark moments in life. Yet, when things go badly, that is not a time to despair, but to trust that God is still with us, even in the darkness. While we may not be able to avoid the tragedies of life, God is with us to help us face whatever ordeals come our way.

After the World Trade Center collapsed from the terrorist attack on September 11, 2001, rescue workers going through the rubble saw two giant beams of steel melted together in the shape of a cross. That cross was a sign of hope to many of the workers who wondered where God was amidst the devastation and death of that awful event. They found their answer in a cross on top of a pile of rubble. God was right there in the middle of it all. Today that cross is in the 9/11 Memorial Museum.

Questions

- Can you think of a difficult time in your life that actually turned out to be a blessing? What was that journey like for you?

- The vicar in *I Heard the Owl Call My Name* talks about "two kinds of naivete," one borne of ignorance and another that acknowledges "man can explain little and still is willing to follow his convictions…" Does this duel description of naivete make sense to you? Does it help you to deal with your doubts and uncertainties about God?

- Romans 8: 28-29 says: "We know that all things work together for good for those who love God, who are called according to his purpose. For those he foreknew he also predestined to be conformed to the image of his Son, in order that he might be the firstborn of a large family." Has there been any bad situation in your life that has turned out for good? Has your suffering ever brought you closer to God or given your life a renewed purpose?

Prayer: How brief is our span of time compared with the time since you created the universe. How tiny we are compared with the enormity of your universe. How trivial are our concerns compared with the complexity of your universe. How stupid we are compared to the genius of your universe. Yet, during every minute and every second of our lives you are present, within and around us. You give your whole and undivided attention to each and every one of us. Our concerns are your concerns. And you are infinitely patient with our stupidity. I thank you with all my heart, knowing that my thanks are worthless compared to your greatness. – Bishop Fulbert of Chartres (970 – 1028)

LESSON 11

WHEN YOU CAN'T CHALLENGE GOD
(Chapters 32 – 35)

Herbert Howells, the English choral composer, was living a placid but successful life as a teacher at the Royal College of Music in London and Music Director at St. Paul's Girls' School. In September 1935, his life was abruptly shattered when his nine-year-old son Michael contracted spinal meningitis during a family holiday. The boy died in London three days later. Howells was deeply affected by the tragedy and suffered depression. His faith, which was never strong, began to evaporate.

Just when he was at a breaking point, he received a request for a new hymn tune in the morning post. The text was written by the seventeenth century German poet Joachim Neander and had been recently translated by Robert Bridges. The words of the poem spoke to Howells and lifted him out of his depression. He is said to have written the tune over breakfast. In memory of his son, he named it *Michael*. The hymn titled "All My Hope on God is Founded" is found in many hymnals today. Here is the opening verse:

All my hope on God is founded; he doth still my trust renew.
Me through change and chance he guideth only good and only true.
God unknown, he alone, calls my heart to be his own.[1]

Sometimes in a conversation with a friend, or reading a book or poem, or on a nature hike, or sailing on the sea, or in a service of worship, we find the resolve to persevere when life falls apart. It is an experience of grace where we find strength for the journey.

Thus far in our study, Job has not found any strength for his life. He is physically hurting and spiritually confused. He cannot reconcile how a just God could allow such suffering to come upon him. There seems nothing for him except death and decay. He is a man without hope.

Gary Nicolosi

Elihu's Challenge to Job (Chapters 32 – 33)

Job's friends have exhausted their arguments. As the discussion between Job and his friends progressed over several days, people gathered around them to hear what was being said. Now a young man by the name of Elihu speaks up. Up to this point, Elihu's youth has prevented him from speaking or interrupting his elders (32:4). However, sensing that Job's three friends have no more to say, he addresses the group in an angry tone.

Elihu is upset because Job has chosen to blame God rather than look at his own character (32:5-9). The young man attempts to give a fair and objective presentation of the matter, even as he continues to defend the prevailing doctrine that sin and suffering are connected. He focuses on the disciplinary role of suffering: God uses suffering to discipline and instruct faithful people who may require correction.

Elihu is sincere and speaks from the heart. He also acknowledges that he is a mere mortal "formed from a piece of clay" (33:6) and therefore he recognizes his fallibility and limitations. He calls Job by name, which indicates a heartfelt concern for him. He listens attentively to Job's words and even summarizes Job's arguments. As he lays out his own case, he does not want to misquote or misinterpret Job. He wants to be sure he understands Job's words and meaning accurately (33:8-11). He does not want to speak without first understanding what has been said.

Elihu is intent on upholding the sovereignty of God: that God is greater than our understanding, and that human beings at best understand the ways of God partially but never fully (33:12). When God speaks, we may not hear what God is saying, or we may misinterpret the message. Sometimes we think God is silent when he is speaking in ways we don't perceive (33:14). For example, God may be speaking to us through another person, or through events, or through our experiences, or through nature. Verbal communication, Elihu maintains, is only one of many ways God speaks to us.

According to the prophet Isaiah, God's ways are beyond our ability to comprehend: "For as the heavens are higher than the earth, so my ways are higher than your ways, my thoughts than your thoughts" (Is. 55:9). God is greater than our understanding, and it would be foolish for any of us to put God in a box and claim definitively to know God's purpose. With God we are always pursuing truth but never fully possessing it.

In grappling with why his own Jewish people did not embrace the Gospel, St. Paul acknowledged this mystery. In Chapters 9 through 11 in his Letter to the Romans, Paul concludes: "O the depth of the riches and wisdom and knowledge of God! How unsearchable are his judgments and how inscrutable his ways! 'For who has known the mind of the Lord? Or who has been his counselor?'" (Rom. 11:33-34). In the end, as Isaiah and Paul understood, there are some things we do not know and may never know about God's ways. Where knowledge falls short, faith begins.

Elihu goes on to maintain that God speaks to us in three ways: through dreams, suffering, and angels.

God speaks through dreams (33:15-18). In Scripture God often communicates his will to someone in a dream – think of Joseph in Matthew's Gospel, for example (Mt. 1:18-24; 2:13,19). However, we must be careful about dreams because they are never to take the place of Scripture or the teachings of the Church. Always evaluate dreams by Scripture and Church teaching, and seek the counsel of a spiritual director or wise friend.

God speaks through suffering (33:19-22). Suffering may be a wake-up call from God to get serious about our lives. Or it may be an invitation to evaluate our priorities. Often pain is the way God gets our attention. Moreover, suffering is an opportunity for us to build character and to trust God more deeply. When we have problems and handle them with patience, we develop spiritual maturity. Patience is standing up to the problems of life without falling apart.

God speaks to us through angels (33:23-24). Angels are messengers from God who give us a word to believe or a message on how to live. Sometimes it is through angels that we are reminded to live a faithful life. We mainly think of angels as spiritual beings, but they also can be human beings. We may be able to think of angels in our own lives who have helped us through tough times or given us the encouragement we needed at just the right moment. A church deacon, for example, used to refer to "his angel" meaning a generous but anonymous benefactor who would donate funds to assist people in need. If we think about it, there are many kinds of angels in our lives, both known and unknown.

Gary Nicolosi

The Justice and Sovereignty of God (Chapters 34 – 35)

Elihu now becomes more theological in his argument. He deals with Job's claim that, given his treatment by God, there is no profit in trying to please him (34:9). Elihu responds that God cannot treat the righteous and the wicked in the same way; otherwise there would be no benefit in pleasing God. In other words, what is the motivation for being faithful if both the wicked and the righteous are treated the same way? Why be faithful at all?

Elihu claims that if God treated the just and the unjust the same way, then God would be unjust. If God is unjust, then there really is no God at all – at least not the God who guarantees a moral universe. For Elihu, the idea of an unjust God is absurd. God has to be just and therefore justice must prevail in the world (34:10-12). Otherwise, the world would fall into chaos. God would never pervert justice by treating the wicked the same as the righteous. God "shows no partiality to nobles, nor regards the rich more than the poor…" (34:19).

Despite the logic of this argument, in the New Testament, Jesus teaches that God "makes the sun rise on the evil and on the good, and sends rain on the righteous and on the unrighteous" (Mt. 5:45). This certainly does not mean the absence of justice in the world or any lack of accountability for wrongdoers. Jesus speaks of a day of judgment for the wheat and the weeds, the sheep and the goats (Mt. 13:24-30; 25:31-46). In this life, however, God blesses indiscriminately.

Since there is no belief in an afterlife, Elihu argues that mortals should respond to the ways of God with humility and deference. If there are things we cannot understand, we must still worship and adore, not rebel and reject. "Know who you are, mortal," Elihu says to Job. The mystery of God can never be fully known by any human being, and it is both folly and arrogance to attempt to try. He dismisses Job's arguments: "Job speaks without knowledge; his words are without insight. …For he adds rebellion to his sin; he claps his hands among us, and multiplies his words against God" (34:35,37).

Elihu is not done. He continues his speech in Chapter 35, defending the sovereignty of God. He decries human beings as presumptuous who dare to question God's ways. He declares: "Surely God does not hear an empty cry, nor does the Almighty regard it" (35:13). For Elihu, God is in control of the world. Human beings only do what God allows. Notice that Elihu refers to God as the "Almighty." Elihu is determined to maintain God as all-powerful in the oversight of the world (35:5-7). No mortal should question the sovereignty of God.

He goes on to say that God gives us "strength in the night" (35:10). No matter how dark things might be in our lives, with God there is always hope. God reaches out to our pain. We never suffer alone: God is with us, in us, and for us, sustaining and strengthening us for what we have to bear. God may not take away our suffering, but he sees us through it. We never walk alone.

The great mistake of many people, according to Elihu, is that we bargain with God in our prayer. We cry out to God, but only for deliverance. When we suffer, we don't want a way forward but a way out. However, prayer is not a bargaining tool or negotiating technique. Nor is it a magic way of alleviating our pain. In one of his most incisive essays on prayer, C.S. Lewis wrote: "For prayer is request. The essence of request, as distinct from compulsion, is that it may or may not be granted."[2] We can make our request boldly to God, but then we need to live with the answer – yes, no, wait – always trusting God even when we do not understand his ways. Jesus gave us the perfect model for prayer in time of adversity. In his agony in the garden, he cried out, "My Father, if it is possible, let this cup pass from me; yet not what I want but what you want" (Mt. 26:39). We pray that God will take the cup of suffering from us, but then we submit to God's will. This is a challenge for the best of us. However, in the religious life, we live by faith and not by sight; we trust even without clear and convincing evidence. In fact, as we grow in the religious life, miracles may become less frequent, as C.S. Lewis acknowledged.[3]

For Reflection

Cardinal Terrence Cooke served as the Roman Catholic Archbishop of New York. He was a quiet and gentle man, but with a deep trust in God that sustained him at a time of social and religious upheaval both in society and the church. In 1983, he was diagnosed with leukemia and

Gary Nicolosi

by the end of the summer it was apparent that he would soon die. Days before his death, October 9, 1983, Cardinal Cooke issued a pastoral letter to his flock in which he said: "The 'gift of life' is no less beautiful when it is accompanied by illness, weakness, hunger or poverty, mental or physical handicaps, loneliness or old age. Indeed, at these times, human life gains extra splendor as it requires our special care, concern and reverence. It is through the weakest of human vessels that the Lord continues to reveal the power of His love."[4]

The Cardinal lived and died what he believed. There was something deeply noble about the way he met death, trusting in the God who created him, sustained him and would now receive him into heaven.

At the same time that Cardinal Cooke was battling cancer, so was my cousin Phyllis. She was diagnosed with an aggressive form of breast cancer that would take her life on December 29, 1983. Nothing the doctors tried had any effect on the cancer – not cobalt treatments, a new form of chemotherapy, or two mastectomies. The cancer continued to spread relentlessly throughout her body.

Even so, Phyllis was a fighter who loved life. She persisted in her struggle to be cured, strengthened by her Catholic faith. Following the advice the Welsh poet Dylan Thomas gave to his dying father, she did "not go gentle into that good night."

Throughout her ordeal, Phyllis never felt sorry for herself. She bore her suffering with a love that touched those closest to her. Her cancer was a killer, but it never killed her spirit. At one stage in her illness, she was active in helping other cancer patients cope with their suffering. Not without tears, Phyllis openly shared her struggles in the conviction that others who were struggling like her need not struggle alone. She was not content to die with dignity but to live in faith. In bearing her suffering with love, Phyllis gave love to others. When she died, there were tears to be sure from those who loved her, but there was also a recognition of a life well lived. In her "sickness unto death," we had a glimpse of salvation.

Questions

- Thinking back, can you recall times that you sensed God speaking to you? What are the ways that God has spoken to you?

- The sovereignty or mystery of God means that God's ways are not our ways. How difficult is it for you to accept God's sovereignty in your life, especially when things don't go as planned or expected?

- How does faith, or trusting God, help you when you are going through a difficult time?

Prayer: Watch, dear Lord, with those who wake or watch or weep tonight, and give your angels charge over those who sleep. Tend your sick ones, O Lord, Jesus Christ, rest your weary ones, bless your dying ones, soothe your suffering ones, shield your joyous ones, and all for your love's sake. – St. Augustine of Hippo (354 – 430)

LESSON 12

WHEN GOD KEEPS SILENT
(JOB 36 – 41)

Shortly after World War II, three rabbis were debating whether God existed or not. The Holocaust had shaken the faith of many of their synagogue members. How could the Jews be God's chosen people and yet undergo so much suffering, not just from Hitler and the Nazis but throughout history? The discussion was intense, but they finally agreed that in view of the evidence, God could not possibly exist. When they concluded their discussion, they adjourned to say evening prayer.

The rabbis were torn between the head and the heart. Their heads – their intellects – told them that it was impossible to reconcile a loving God with a suffering world, especially one where God's chosen people suffered so horrifically. On the other hand, their heart still believed in God. They could no more abandon God than they could abandon themselves.

The harsh reality of this world leads some people to doubt God's existence. A friend of Sigmund Freud, who was a cancer specialist, got into a conversation with the famous psychiatrist. He said that when he died and came to the throne of the Almighty, he would take with him a cancerous human bone and demand an explanation.

Is God really in control of things? The question is as old as humanity's faith in a Supreme Being. In darker moments, the question raised by the Christian philosopher Boethius (480 – 524) becomes insistent: If God is righteous, why evil? Boethius answered: Either God wishes to prevent evil but cannot, in which case God is just but not omnipotent. Or God can prevent evil but does not want to, in which case God is omnipotent but not just.[1]

Theologians over the centuries have responded differently to Boethius' dilemma. Some theologians have maintained the absolute sovereignty of God who controls or even micromanages every aspect of human existence, the good and the evil. Others have taught that God created the world but is not involved in its daily affairs. Still others have argued that a moral God is not able to control all the evil and suffering in the world. Most theologians have sought to hold in balance God's sovereignty, human freedom and the natural order of the world without ever fully resolving the difficulties.

Many people are not sure about God but are quite sure about evil. It haunts us, stares us in the face, and dares us to come to terms with it.

All the arguments by Job and his friends led to a stalemate. It is time for God to speak for himself. This is the moment we have waited for. What will God say in his defense? Could God not have made a better world if he is truly all-powerful? Does he want to make a better world if he is truly all-moral? God, what have you to say for yourself?

Elihu, the young man who speaks after Job's friends, sets the stage for what God will say. God is sovereign, Elihu says, and it is not for human beings to challenge his wisdom or ways. He tells Job that he can't believe in God's greatness and then question his judgments. God's power and God's goodness are held in tension, not always easily reconcilable. The faithful person lives with this tension rather than insisting on any definitive resolution. God, after all, is Creator of the universe. How can any creature claim to understand fully the mystery of God's ways? They are beyond human comprehension (37:1-24).

The essence of the religious life is to trust God in the face of things we cannot understand and dare not accept. The human mind can go only so far in understanding the ways of God. At some point, we have to say to the Lord, "I believe; help my unbelief" (Mk. 9:24).

The Lord's First Challenge (Chapters 38:1 – 40:5)

After Elihu's speech, God makes his appearance. But rather than answer Job's questions, God turns the tables and poses questions to Job. God responds to the mystery of suffering with the mystery of himself.

God throws out question after question to Job – eighty-three of them. Job is able to answer none. In effect, God says to Job: Who do you think you are questioning me? I am the Creator of the world. I gave the universe its shape and distinct character, and the moral and physical laws that govern it. I am before the beginning of time and I will be when there is no more time. Everything that exists is created by me and sustained by me. I am God, the Almighty, the omnipotent, the sovereign Creator of all that exists. I answer to no one! (38:1-12).

There are thirty-nine questions in Chapter 38, twenty questions in Chapters 39:1 – 40:2, and twenty-four questions in Chapters 40:6 – 41:34. And Job can't answer a single one! He was expecting answers from God. Instead God fires questions at him. Their purpose is not to humiliate Job but to make a point: the mystery and grandeur of creation requires the might and wisdom of a God who could create such a universe. In contrast, human beings are weak, finite, fallible and limited in understanding.

God takes Job on an incomprehensible journey of creation where human understanding gives way to the mystery of existence. God directs Job's attention to the animal kingdom. Is that something Job is able to oversee? God questions him about the beasts of the earth, but Job knows none of the answers. If Job doesn't even know his own world, then how can he know God's? In the face of God's majesty, there is only mystery. Explanation gives way to silence.

God concludes his first speech by asking, "Shall a faultfinder contend with the Almighty?" (40:2). Job's response is one of humble submission and acknowledgement that God's ways are beyond his understanding. He then does something for the first time. Job admits his inadequacy to challenge God: "See, I am of small account; what shall I answer you? I lay my hand on my mouth" (40:4).

The Lord's Second Challenge (40:6 – 41:34)

Job assumed equality with God, and therefore the right to challenge God's judgments. God replies: "Will you put me in the wrong? Will you condemn me that you may be justified?" (40:8). In other words, the creature dare not question the Creator.

God selects two creatures about which to question Job: the Behemoth (40:15) and the Leviathan (41:1). There is scholarly debate about these animals. Some scholars believe the Behemoth is likely the hippopotamus. An adult hippo weighs up to 8,000 pounds and has armor-like skin impossible to penetrate in Job's day. The Leviathan is most likely the crocodile – a man-eater feared in the ancient world. Hunters seldom tried to capture or kill a crocodile because their weapons would not penetrate its tough skin.

Both the crocodile and the hippopotamus were considered beyond taming or domestication. If human beings are unable to control these fierce animals, then how can they claim to question God who created them?

Job concludes that he is not equal to God, either in understanding or power. And God is not his servant who must respond to Job's questions. God is mystery beyond our finite minds. Theologians refer to God as Being – pure "is-ness," the source of all that exists and (unimaginable to us) beyond time and space. In the Book of Exodus, God tells Moses, "I AM WHO I AM" (Ex. 3:14). In other words, trying to imagine God without God first revealing himself is impossible.

In the end, God says nothing about Job's suffering, nor does God address the problem of divine justice. Job gets neither a bill of indictment nor a verdict of innocence. He gets no answer to his *why* questions – only a series of questions from God that he cannot answer.

God's response does not satisfy us moderns. We demand answers to our questions. Sometimes we do receive answers, but often, like Job, we encounter the incomprehensibility of a sovereign, loving and just God who creates a less than perfect world that includes suffering and injustice. Our response should be neither to limit God's power nor question God's goodness. The vindication of God does not come about through philosophical speculation but by faith – that God is good even when we experience suffering and injustice. As God says to Job: "Will you ever put me in the wrong? Will you condemn me that you may be justified?" (40:9). It is not for the creature to question the Creator. After all, God upheld the universe before us and will uphold the universe after us. We are not in a position to question God. All we can affirm is that God is sovereign!

For Reflection

When I served a church in Lancaster County, Pennsylvania, I got to know Sarah. She was a former Mennonite who now attended a megachurch that taught "name it and claim theology" – a belief that with enough faith in God, anything is possible. I found that theology simplistic and even damaging. Still, I liked Sarah. She was a bubbly, vivacious person with a smile on her face. She was always praising God. And yet, I was suspicious of her. I thought: what if someday something tragic happens to Sarah? She won't be able to cope with it. Her positive, upbeat attitude will quickly dissipate.

Well, something tragic did happen to Sarah. She developed a debilitating illness that made her completely dependent on those around her. Thankfully, she had a loving husband and six dear children to support her. At first, Sarah and her friends from church prayed for a miracle that would restore her bodily health. They prayed and prayed but none came. Finally, Sarah had to face the fact that her prayers and those of her many friends were not being answered, at least not in the way they would have liked. This was a crossroads in her life. It was easy to praise God for a miracle, but could she praise God in her suffering? She saw before her a choice: would she be "an embittered cripple" for the rest of her life or would she praise God in the midst of her pain?

Sarah chose praise. She came to the growing certainty that God is always present, whatever our bodily condition; and that we need to resist approaching God as a bottle of aspirins rather than as the answer to a lost world. Amid her suffering, Sarah discovered the importance of praise. She began to understand that God does not witness to the world by taking us out of suffering. God witnesses by demonstrating his grace through our suffering. He allows our weakness to reveal his strength in adversity.

A person quite different from Sarah was Bishop John A.T. Robinson, one of the great scholars of the Church of England. In June of 1983, Bishop Robinson discovered he had terminal cancer. He and his wife wrote a letter to friends to share with them the sad diagnosis but also a word of comfort. They concluded with a phrase from Dag Hammarskjold: "For all that has been – Thanks! To all that shall be – Yes!"[2]

John Robinson, English Bishop, Cambridge scholar, renowned theologian was not all that different from Sarah. In life as in death, they both trusted the Lord. They accepted that we who are called to trust God in life are also called to trust God at death. We who are called to praise God in health are also called to praise God in sickness. Jesus leads us to himself by way of the cross. The road to suffering is the surest way to

Jesus. These are difficult words, but they are true. Suffering is redemptive if united to Jesus who suffered and died for us.

Questions

- In the Book of Job God presents us with faith and mystery rather than clear-cut answers. If you had your choice, would you prefer a religion that gave you all the answers in a rational and systematic way or a religion of mystery and miracle that accepts the supernatural and incomprehensibility of life?

- If God is righteous, why evil? Either God wishes to prevent evil but cannot, in which case God is not all-powerful. Or God can prevent evil but does not want to, in which case God is all-powerful but not just. How would you answer Boethius' dilemma of a just God who is all-powerful but creates a less than perfect world?

- Today human beings are discovering a growing number of answers to the questions posed by God to Job. Science can explain the world in ways unimagined by previous generations. What are the implications for faith as science answers the questions that faith once thought mysterious? Are there any questions science cannot answer?

Prayer: Dear Lord, it seems that you are so madly in love with your creatures that you could not live without us. So you created us; and then, when we turned away from you, you redeemed us. Yet, you are God and so have no need of us. Your greatness is made no greater by our creation; your power is made no stronger by our redemption. You have no duty to care for us, no debt to re-pay us. It is love, and love alone, which moves you. – St. Catherine of Siena (1347 – 1380)

LESSON 13

WHEN FAITH IS VINDICATED
(JOB 42)

When my wife Heather discovered she was pregnant, we began to pray every day for a healthy baby. For eight months we prayed faithfully, and for eight months we had no reason to think that the baby in Heather's womb was other than perfectly normal.

After Heather gave birth and held our daughter Allison in her arms, we sensed that something was not quite right. It was Allison's eyes... there was something about them. With the nurse present, Heather said to me, "It looks like she has Down syndrome." The nurse left the room without saying a word. A short time later the doctor came in and told us what we suspected: Allison had Down syndrome.

It is impossible to describe the feelings that swell within you when you are told such news. There was none of the usual joy that accompanies a birth. It was more like a death to our hopes and dreams for our daughter. Breaking the news to our parents was especially difficult.

What made things worse was that on the day Heather was set to leave the hospital, Allison had to remain. We had to leave our baby behind as we went home. It was just too much for us to bear. We couldn't go home to a nursery without our baby. What should we do next?

At the end of the lesson, I will share more of our story. For now, I can tell you that we found ourselves asking, "Why?" – Why did this happen to us? And like Job, we could not think of an answer.

The Book of Job is the story of one man's anger with God. Job has suffered beyond what most of us can even imagine, losing everything of value: his children, health and wealth as well as his stellar reputation in the community. Remarkably, though, Job remained steadfastly loyal to God, even as he questioned God's ways.

God, in turn, refused to placate Job with answers. The Creator would not justify his ways to his creatures. Instead God asked Job a series of unrelenting questions that Job could not answer. Job finally came to realize that his accusations against God were presumptuous. In the end, the mystery of suffering lies in the mystery of God.

Job's Changed Attitude (Chapter 42)

After God finishes his speeches, Job develops a new understanding of the greatness and majesty of God. He humbly confesses, "I know that you can do all things, and that no purpose of yours can be thwarted... Therefore I have uttered what I did not understand, things too wonderful for me, which I did not know." (42:2, 3b). Job has a new appreciation of God's hidden plans and a greater awareness of his own fallibility. He even says, "Therefore I despise myself, and repent in dust and ashes" (42:6).

To repent means both a change of mind and a change of life. Job now re-thinks all he has said in questioning God. His fundamental perspective changes as he realizes that God's ways are indeed beyond our understanding.

After Job's confession, God sets his sights on his three friends. He issues a divine reprimand. They have defended the traditional view that suffering is the result of sin, but this is not always the case (42:7). God requires the three of them to offer seven bulls and seven rams as a burnt offering for misrepresenting him (42:8). This is a huge offering, clearly indicating the degree of offense involved. While they were in good faith, they tarnished the goodness of God and misrepresented God's ways to a man who was suffering without fault. Job prays for his friends that God would restore them to his fellowship (42:10). Since Job forgave his friends, God does too.

God now restores Job's losses and gives him twice as much as he had before (42:10). Job's friends, relatives and acquaintances give him gold and silver for a new start (42:11). He begins his business again, purchases more animals, hires servants and is blessed with ten additional children (42:12). Moreover, the Lord restores Job's health and doubles the length of his life (42:16-17).

None of this should mean that material blessings always follow undeserved suffering. What the Book of Job tells us is that God holds sovereign and loving sway over every human life. Therefore, God can be trusted in all things, even when we may not see a purpose to our pain or any vindication against injustice. God always writes the last chapter of our lives, but the last chapter may not be written in this life. Still, Christians know the end of the story. As Billy Graham famously said, "I have read the last page of the Bible. It is all going to turn out all right."

As we conclude the Book of Job, there are nine points to ponder. Together they provide a pathway to strength in adversity.

First, adversity happens for reasons beyond our understanding, but we can move forward in faith. Can we with our finite minds fully reconcile a just and loving God with a world of injustice and suffering? Scripture itself sets up the issue through the suffering of Job. He is faithful, devout and pious, but he suffers terribly and demands to know why. God, however, does not respond to Job's questions and refuses to share the reasons for his suffering. Many of us may be offended by this God, who is decidedly not warm and fuzzy. The point to be grasped for our own good – psychologically and spiritually – is that God's ways are not our ways (Is. 55:8-9). We are invited to take our cue from Job who reluctantly comes to grips with God's awe-inspiring sovereignty, but also moves forward in faith. Christians would want to take their cue from St. Paul who experienced immense difficulties in his ministry, and yet was steadfast in his loyalty and commitment to Jesus (2 Cor. 4:8-11; 11:22-29; 2 Tim. 6-8). Paul resolved to persevere in the midst of hardships, even when he did not understand the reasons for them. Sometimes the only thing we can do is persevere and not give in to despair. We refuse to allow pain to have the last word in our lives. A prayer attributed to St. Ignatius Loyola puts it this way: "Dearest Lord, teach me to be generous. Teach me to serve you as you deserve; to give and not to count the cost; to fight and not to heed the wounds; to toil and not to seek for rest; to labor and not to ask for any reward save that of knowing that I am doing your will." In other words, we move forward in faith living in God's will, regardless of any suffering that comes our way.

Second, adversity calls us to trust God even when our world is in disarray. Life can be tough for the best of us, and in times of crisis, it is difficult to trust God. We may question whether God exists, or if he does, whether he even cares about us. For all his suffering, Job refused to curse God, even as he questioned his ways. There is something heroic about Job, as there is with Habakkuk and the other Hebrew prophets who experienced tragic times yet held fast to faith in God. The same is true in the New Testament as Christians were persecuted by the Roman Empire. Writing to a suffering church, St. Peter exhorts Christians "not to be surprised at the fiery ordeal that is taking place among you… But rejoice insofar as you are sharing Christ's sufferings, so that you may also be glad and shout for joy when his glory is revealed. …Therefore, let those suffering in accordance with God's will entrust themselves to a faithful Creator, while continuing to do good" (1 Pet. 4:12, 13, 19). St. Teresa of Avila, who greatly suffered as a result of her reform of the Carmelites, counseled her sisters: "Let nothing disturb you. Let nothing frighten you. All things pass. God does not change. Patience achieves everything. Whoever has God lacks nothing. God alone suffices."

Third, adversity forces us to acknowledge that life is unfair, but with God there is always hope. Life was not fair to Job, a just man who lost his health, wealth and children. And, to one degree or another, life is not fair to us either. Things happen that we do not plan or want. We get diagnosed with heart disease or cancer. We find ourselves caring for an aging parent, or losing our job, or coping with money issues, or struggling with depression, diabetes, Parkinson's, loss of sight, hearing or mobility. Sadly, I could go on. None of these things may be fair, but they happen. The lesson from Job is to keep your faith and persevere as you are able in the face of life's unfairness. Paul, who was awaiting execution in a Roman prison and who had suffered much as a Christian, never wavered in his faith in Christ or his hope for the future. In his last letter before death, he wrote: "As for me, I am already being poured out as a libation, and the time of my departure has come. I have fought the good fight, I have finished the race, I have kept the faith. From now on there is reserved for me the crown of righteousness…" (2 Tim. 4:6-8). Paul knew, as we should know, that whatever happens to us in this life, Jesus is Lord and God is sovereign. Thomas Merton, who went through some very dark times spiritually and emotionally as a monk, nonetheless prayed to God: "Therefore, I will trust you always, though I may seem to be lost and in the shadow of death. I will not fear, for you are ever with me, and you will never leave me to face my perils alone."[1] At the end of our journey, there is God. He is our hope even when life goes wrong.

Fourth, adversity – and how we handle it – can inspire others. Faithful Christians who suffer can be inspirations to others who are experiencing their own pain. Of all the saints, the martyrs are at the top of the hierarchy; after all, they suffered and died for Jesus. While awaiting execution in the Tower of London for refusing to take the oath that King Henry VIII was the Supreme Head of the Church of England, Sir Thomas More wrote to his beloved daughter Margaret: "Do not let your heart be troubled over anything that shall happen to me in this world. Nothing can come but what God wills. And I am sure that whatever that be; however bad it may seem, it shall indeed be the best." More remained positive and hopeful even in prison, not because he expected a different outcome, but because his faith in God was unwavering. Today, Sir Thomas More is Saint Thomas More – a declaration by the Roman Catholic Church that More's life and death is an inspiration to all of us who value conscience, character and personal integrity.

Fifth, adversity can make us more compassionate toward others. Suffering can make us more compassionate and less judgmental. As the noted Roman Catholic priest Henri Nouwen wrote in his book *The Wounded Healer,* you become a wounded healer because you yourself have been wounded. Only the one who has suffered can enter into the suffering of others. St. Paul says that one of the purposes of tribulation is that we might be better able to comfort those in trouble (2 Cor. 1:4). Unless you have known pain, you really can't show comfort to those in pain. Take Mother Teresa, for example. Although we did not know it when she was alive, in her journals published after her death, she reveals her deep depression even as she continued her charitable work in the Calcutta slums. Although suffering the dark night of the soul, she prayed: "Make us worthy, Lord, to serve our fellow human beings throughout the world who live and die in poverty and hunger. Give them through our hands this day their daily bread, and by our understanding love, give peace and joy."[2] Along with her faith, it was her compassion and commitment to the poor that sustained her in the darkest moments of her life.

Sixth, adversity drives us to re-examine our priorities. Suffering and adversity help us get our priorities in order. We gain perspective through our pain and come to realize what is important in life. Many people, for example, have reordered their priorities after a medical diagnosis or a near-death experience. In May 2005, Eugene O'Kelly, who was the CEO of KPMG, one of the largest accounting firms in the United States, learned that he had inoperable, incurable brain cancer, and was told he would die in six months or less. He died, in fact, on September 10, 2005. Before he died O'Kelly authored a book, which was published posthumously, about his reflections on his life and pending death. The book is titled, *Chasing Daylight: How My Forthcoming Death Transformed My Life*. O'Kelly's illness prompted him to re-examine his priorities and values. He drew a map of relationships in his life as a series of five concentric circles. His wife was at the center, then his children, on through family and close friends, and finally close business associates. He realized that he had spent far too much time in the outer circles and not enough on the inner ones. His lifestyle had not been in harmony with his priorities. We may be more fortunate than O'Kelly. Suffering may not end our life, but it can change us for the better as we examine whether our values and priorities are in harmony with our beliefs and behavior. James 4:14 tells us: "For you are a mist that appears for a little while and then vanishes." In the short time we have on this earth, we should savor life, be a blessing to others, and live faithfully according to our circumstances. The Jesuit mystic Anthony De Mello wisely counseled: "Peace is only found in yes."[3] Yes to Jesus, yes to doing his will, yes to walking in his way, and yes to following in the way of love.

Seventh, adversity can accelerate spiritual growth. So often we think that God blesses us in the good times but abandons us in the tough times. However, the spiritually mature person understands that God is with us in all the ups-and-downs of life. The trials and troubles of life require endurance if we are to draw closer to God. The Epistle to James addresses the importance of endurance in our suffering: "As an example of suffering and patience, beloved, take the prophets who spoke in the name of the Lord. Indeed we call blessed those who showed endurance. You have heard of the endurance of Job, and you have seen the purpose of the Lord, how the Lord is compassionate and merciful" (Jas. 5:10-11). The El Salvador Jesuit and martyr Ignacio Martin-Baro, who with five other Jesuits and two workers were murdered by a death squad in the early morning of November 16, 1989, wrote before his death of his precarious situation: "There are truths that can only be discovered through suffering or from the critical vantage point of extreme situations."[4] Personal and spiritual growth often happen through suffering when we move out of our comfort zone, stretch ourselves, and venture into new horizons which may disturb us, challenge us, or even threaten us. It is through such experiences that God sheds light on ourselves and our world.

Eight, adversity can make us honestly humble. When everything is going well in our lives, we may act like we don't need God. Yet, at some point our world may come crashing down and it is then we feel the need for God. Adversity shakes us from our self-sufficiency and helps us to see ourselves as we really are – mortal, frail and fallible human beings who may die from a virus we can't even see. There is an old saying: "Some people never look up until they are flat on their backs." St. Paul wrote that he experienced extreme adversity so that he might not trust in himself but in the Lord who has the power to raise the dead (2 Cor. 1:9). Cardinal Avery Dulles was perhaps America's greatest Roman Catholic theologian, a brilliant mind and gentle soul. In his last years of life, his polio, which he had contracted as a youth, returned and crippled his body. This once giant of a man was now helpless. In his last public lecture, which was read by an associate because of his inability to speak, Dulles ended with these words: "As I become increasingly paralyzed and unable to speak, I can identify with the many paralytics and mute persons in the gospels, grateful for the loving and skillful care I receive and for the hope of everlasting life in Christ. If the Lord now calls me to a period of weakness, I know well that his power can be made perfect in infirmity. 'Blessed be the name of the Lord!'"[5]

Ninth, adversity can build character. Like physical health, there is no spiritual excellence without exertion. Growth involves moving out of our comfort zone, refusing to remain static, and being willing to stretch ourselves, even when the cost is high. St. Paul wrote, "Suffering produces endurance, and endurance produces character, and character produces hope, and hope does not disappoint us…"(Rom. 5:3-4). Think of Charles Colson, Special Counsel to President Nixon. Once known as Nixon's "hatched man," Colson pleaded guilty to obstruction of justice during the Watergate scandal and served seven months in a federal prison. And yet, the result of that experience led to a profound Christian conversion which he wrote about in his book *Born Again*. Once released from prison, Colson began Prison Fellowship International, an organization that has helped thousands of prisoners and their families. His books, lectures and witness made him one of the best known Christians in the world, and in 1993 he received the Templeton Prize for Progress in Religion. Or take financier Michael Milken, the junk bond king of Wall Street, who served time in federal prison for violating U.S. security laws. While in prison Milken was diagnosed with prostate cancer. That diagnosis changed his life. He renewed his Jewish heritage which included a commitment to charitable giving. After his release from prison he set up a foundation to fund medical research into curing melanoma and prostate cancer. In November 2004, *Fortune Magazine* called Milken "the man who changed medicine" – his work in medical research had become that influential. Colson and Milken are very different personalities, but they are proof that suffering can change our character and bring out the best in us.

The Book of Job has inspired readers over the centuries. It has also frustrated readers, since it does not answer the burning question that the book itself poses: why we suffer. For that reason it is bound to frustrate people accustomed to answers to their every question. In the end, however, Job is not a book that rationalizes our experience but calls us to live by faith. Its message is fairly simple to state: We may never know the *why* of suffering, so our task becomes not to know but to trust. We are called to trust that God is good all the time, even when things are bad. And while that is easy to say, we know from experience, it is hard to accept. Still, in

God's strength, we can live with this assurance: although we may never know the reason why we suffer in this life, someday we will.

For Reflection

After Heather and I left the hospital without our baby, we found it too painful to go home immediately. So we went to our favorite park. It was a golden October day in upstate New York. The sun was shining and the leaves were at their peak. We got out of our car, and sat before a waterfall. There were no words between us. What could we say? But then, after about fifteen minutes of silence, something remarkable happened. An incredible peace came over me. The anxiety I felt about the future seemed to vanish. I turned to Heather and said, "It's going to be all right. God has just told me it is going to be all right."

And do you know something? It came out all right. And it has remained all right. And it will always be all right. Allison is now a beautiful young woman. It would be impossible for Heather and me to imagine life without her. She has blessed us and those around her immeasurably. She now lives at Treasure House in Glendale, Arizona, a beautiful and inspiring community for young adults with intellectual and developmental disabilities. On Sunday she assists me as an acolyte at church. She often tells me, "I want to be a priest like my dad." I could not be prouder of my daughter, nor more grateful to have her with me.

Allison has taught me a great truth about life. When tragedy happens in our lives, we have a choice in how we respond. We can focus on the grim reality, or we can take hold of the possibilities, imagine, dream, pray, trust God, think of others, give thanks, and move on with our lives with God's help. We can resolve to live by faith, confident that God is with us every step of the way.

In the novel *The Diary of a Country Priest* by Georges Bernanos, a young priest who has worked tirelessly for his church is dying. In visiting a parishioner, he collapses and falls into delirium. His last words before his death are, "Grace is everywhere."[6]

In the birth of our daughter Allison, Heather and I have come to believe that grace is everywhere. This does not mean an absence of challenges.

Heather and I take it one step at a time with Allison. We need to ensure her well-being for the rest of her life. No matter how much we plan, new issues arise. This is where faith is crucial. Over the years I have learned that when we trust the person of God, we can more easily trust the plan of God. It is not easy, I know, but the first step is to believe that God's love is always and forever. Grace is everywhere.

Questions

- What do you think of the conclusion of the Book of Job? Does this "happy ending" have a ring of truth about it, or does it seem more fantasy than reality?

- What does it mean to live by faith, especially when adversity comes your way?

- Review the nine points on adversity. Is there a particular point that resonates with you? From your experience, what would you add to the list?

Prayer: Lord, my heart is before you. I try, but by myself I can do nothing; do what I cannot. Admit me into your inner room of your love. I ask, I seek, I knock. You who made me seek, make me receive; you who gave me the seeking, give the finding; you who taught the knocking, open to my knock. ...By you I have desire; by you let me have fulfillment. ...Good Lord, do not reject me; I faint with hunger for your love; refresh me with it. Let me be filled with your love, rich in your affection, completely held in your care. Take me and possess me wholly, who with the Father and the Holy Spirit are alone blessed to ages of ages. – St. Anselm of Canterbury (1033 – 1109)

PASTORAL REFLECTIONS

For most of my life, I have had a love affair with Jesus. Though I love my wife and daughter, cherish friends, relatives and colleagues, Jesus has been the central figure in my life. He is the reason I became a priest, dedicated my life to the Church, served parishes across North America, and have this crazy passion to preach the Gospel. Since ordination in June 1983, I have spent four decades sharing Jesus with everyone who would listen, both within and outside the Church. My commitment throughout this time has been to build up the Church as a loving, life-giving community witnessing to the risen Christ and reaching out to people everywhere, no matter who they are or where they are on their journey of faith.

After an early career as a New York attorney practicing labor and criminal law, I finally responded to the call of God to become a priest – a call I first felt in the sixth grade. It was a big risk to leave law practice and study divinity, but it turned out to be the right move.

Most of my time as a priest has been devoted to parish ministry in urban, suburban and rural churches, large and small. I have preached countless sermons, taught hundreds of classes, and led countless seminars on church growth and stewardship across North America. I have baptized well over a thousand people of all ages, and presided at countless weddings and funerals.

All of that makes for a lot of talking, but I have also done a great deal of listening.

During my ministry, I have heard parents pour out their hearts over wayward sons and daughters. The stories, as varied as human experience, contain the usual themes: drug and alcohol abuse, crime, theft from family members, mental illness, and even suicides. I have sat in my church study with men and women who had been successful professionally but were now helplessly dealing with their career in free fall. I have listened to women who have been cheated by their husbands and vice versa. I have heard of shocking tales of family abandonment.

Hospital visits are common place in parish ministry. A priest spends time with family members awaiting the results of emergency surgery, time at the beside of patients who face a long road of recovery, and time with those confronting life's last chapter. I have had to deal with families struggling whether to authorize a loved one to be taken off a respirator, and with patients who have lost limbs. These are times of listening – for what is being said and for what is left unsaid but truly felt.

Hurting people expect to receive from their pastor the right words at the right moment. Isn't that the pastor's job? But what do you say, when you stand next to a child-sized casket and the only sound in the sanctuary are the sobs of a mom and dad and grieving grandparents? In such moments, when words are so inadequate, I prayed for the prompting of God's Spirit: to say the right words in a compassionate and sensitive manner.

That is my prayer now, as we close out this study on adversity and the Book of Job. Are there words that offer insight, encouragement and hope?

During the many times I spent with hurting people, a sentiment almost invariably found its way into the conversation. While not always expressed in these words, it went something like this: "I can't believe this is happening to me…to us…to our family." There is a sense of disbelief that tragedy could strike them and be so personal. Implicit in that sentiment is the question we have wrestled with throughout the Book of Job: "How can an all-powerful and all-loving God allow such things to happen?"

These questions invite all manner of theological and philosophical discussion, as we saw vividly portrayed in the story of Job. But, as we all know from experience, such high-minded debates and speculations can take us only so far. They don't really heal the hurting heart or strengthen the suffering soul. To get there, we need to walk a different path. That's what these pastoral reflections are meant to do.

The Universality of Suffering

All of us grapple with the reality of suffering. It is inadequate and even offensive to respond to suffering with religious clichés, feel-good platitudes and vacuous positive thinking. Reverent silence seems preferable to rationalizing the inexplicable.

In this regard, Roman Catholics have it right when they offer in their prayer *Salve Regina*, sighs of "mourning and weeping in this valley of tears." Life is a "valley of tears" – shocking but true. There are times when adversity takes an enormous toll on us. All of us pass through this "valley of tears," a place where life seems to fall apart.

Love and suffering seem polar opposites to one another. And yet, if God loves the world (Jn. 3:16) and if God is love (1 Jn. 4:16), as Christians claim, then how can such a God possibly allow so much suffering? We may understand when bad or irresponsible people suffer, but what about those who are innocent and responsible? How can suffering be justified for those whose lives are blameless?

We must, of course, begin by being honest with ourselves. Are any of us blameless, no matter how decent and respectable our lives?

The Russian author Alexandre Solzhenitsyn said that the line between good and evil runs through every human heart. We all have sinned and fall short of the glory of God (Rom. 3:23). We commit sins of commission and omission, what we have done and what we have left undone. None of us are blameless. If that is true, then should any of us be surprised by suffering?

When I was a young priest, I had the privilege of hearing Moorhead Kennedy, the last United States ambassador to Iran, speak about terrorism. Ambassador Kennedy knew terrorism firsthand. He had experienced its rage as one of the American hostages in Iran from 1979 to 1981. He also happened to be a Christian and an Episcopalian, who had given the subject of terrorism a great deal of thought while residing as scholar-in-residence at the Cathedral of St. John the Divine in New York. Referring to the provocative title of his book *The Ayatollah in the Cathedral*, Ambassador Kennedy remarked that there is an ayatollah in each of us, dogmatic, proud, arrogant, and intolerant. "We're not much better than our guards," recalled Ambassador Kennedy of the words a marine hostage in Iran spoke as he wondered what he would do if the roles were reversed.

Ambassador Kennedy is right: there is an ayatollah in each of us, and I have seen it in bishops, priests, lay persons and in myself. History has taught us that to be righteously religious can be a very dangerous thing.

The line between good and evil runs through every human heart. There is no use denying Solzhenitsyn's insight. It is true. We all fall short: believers and non-believers, theists and atheists, spiritual, secular and religious people. Therefore, how can any of us expect to avoid some kind of suffering in our lives?

Still, the pain of being human can take an enormous toll on us. Think of your own pain, or the pain of friends and family members. We all have experienced physical, mental, emotional and spiritual suffering – diseases, depression, mental illness, broken marriages, isolation from friends, alienation from the world, the death of loved ones, sexual abuse, drug and alcohol addiction, and so much more.

Look beyond your own pain to the pain of the world where people have experienced unimaginable suffering: the Holocaust, the Gulags of the Soviet Union, the killing fields of Cambodia, the genocide in the old Yugoslavia, the tribal slaughter in Rwanda, the horror of 9/11, the indoctrination camps in China, and now the war in Ukraine.

Then there are the natural disasters that ravage our planet – earthquakes, tornadoes, floods, and fires that have killed hundreds of thousands of people in this century alone. In 2010, the Haitian earthquake killed an estimated 230,00 people, leaving 300,000 injured and one million homeless. In 2004, the Indian Ocean tsunami killed 230,000 people and displaced millions more. Or think of Hurricane Katrina which ravaged the Gulf Coast of the United States in 2005 and killed over 1,800 people. And let us not forget COVID and its variants – a virus that has killed millions and affected the lives of almost every person on the planet. These things shake our confidence in the goodness of the world – and of God – and bring home the reality of evil and suffering.

God's Sovereignty and Human Suffering

How does a believer in an all-powerful, loving God respond to the enormous suffering and injustice in our world?

As we saw vividly throughout the text of the Book of Job, in the Hebrew Scriptures there is no definitive answer to the problem of suffering, only a call to trust God in the midst of things we cannot understand or much less accept. To their everlasting credit, the Hebrew Scriptures neither minimize nor rationalize away the reality of suffering. Even suffering borne in faith does not lessen the pain, though it may help us endure it. And yet, the most faithful believer may still experience the suffering of God-forsakenness.

The psalmist cries out, "My heart is in anguish within me, the terrors of death have fallen upon me. Fear and trembling come upon me, and horror overwhelms me" (Ps. 55:4-5). Suffering may involve a dark night of the soul in which we can only pray, "Out of the depths I cry to you, O Lord" (Ps. 130:1).

Nowhere is the God-forsakenness of suffering laid out with more honesty than in Psalm 88. It is a prayer of utter desolation. Possibly the psalmist suffered from cancer or a deadly skin disease. Deserted by friends, the psalmist feels that even God has deserted him. There is the absence of God in his life, the silence of God to his prayers. What a picture of unrelieved gloom! Still, this is a psalm of hope. Even amid darkest suffering, the psalmist continues to pray. Such prayer, uttered from the anguished depths of the heart, is itself a tribute to the psalmist's faith and his need for God.

In the Book of Ruth, Naomi journeys to a foreign land with her husband and two sons. Her sons marry foreign wives and the family prospers. Then tragedy strikes. Naomi's husband dies followed by her two sons. She is left destitute. Her daughter-in-law Ruth is determined to follow Naomi wherever she goes, but the future seems bleak, if not hopeless for the two of them. In one of the most heartfelt laments in Scripture, Naomi says: "Call me no longer Naomi, call me Mara, for the Almighty has dealt bitterly with me. I went away full, but the Lord has brought me back empty; why call me Naomi when the Lord has dealt harshly with me, and the Almighty has brought calamity upon me?" (Ruth 1:20-21).

As the narrative unfolds, Naomi gets good news. Back in her native land, her daughter-in-law Ruth marries a wealthy relative by the name of Boaz and bears a son. The women in the village rejoice and say to Naomi: "He shall be to you a restorer of life and a nourisher of your old age, for your daughter-in-law who loves you, who is more to you than seven sons, has borne him" (Ruth 4:15). Naomi's grandson would not only be the grandfather of King David, but through his lineage would come Jesus, the Messiah and the Son of God (Mt. 1:5-6,16; Lk. 3:31,37).

The Book of Ruth ends on a happy note, but we know that happy endings don't always happen. The Hebrew Scriptures grapple with suffering, acknowledge it, but in the end find it impossible to reconcile with a sovereign, loving and just God. Either God vindicates his people in this life as with Naomi and Job, or God punishes his people for their infidelity as when Israel was destroyed by the Assyrians and Judah by the Babylonians (Ps. 79). The notion of redemptive suffering is not a theme of the Hebrew Scriptures. Isaiah's Suffering Servant passage (Is. 52:13 – 53:12) is a notable exception. There, the prophet dramatically introduces a theme that otherwise remains undeveloped.

Suffering and Redemption

It is only when we shift our eyes to the New Testament that suffering becomes intelligible. Christianity does not claim redemption from suffering, but redemption through suffering (Heb. 2:10; 5:8). The central thrust of John's Gospel is that Christ came into the world not to live but to die (Jn. 12:27). The message of the New Testament can be summarized in one sentence: Christ's sacrificial death has brought about our redemption.

Made like us in every way except sin, the Christ who is nailed to the cross is a profoundly vulnerable human being. He is a man who knows hunger and thirst. He struggles with temptation. He feels the failures and frustrations of a broken world, "a man of suffering and acquainted with infirmity" (Is. 53:3). He is a man who sheds tears at the tomb of Lazarus. His sweat is like drops of blood in the Garden of Gethsemane where he begs his Father to "remove this cup from me" (Mk. 14:36). When his friends had forsaken him, the religious leaders condemned him, and the Roman soldiers crucified him, he cried out from the cross quoting Psalm 22: "My God, my God, why have you forsaken me?" (Ps. 22:1).

The death of Jesus provides us with an understanding of suffering. If there was anyone who did not deserve to suffer, it was Jesus. And yet, he was tortured to death on a cross. He cried to his Father for relief, but none came. The crucifixion is one of the most disturbing incidents about Christianity, and yet it is at the heart of our faith. There is a mystery here about why God who loved his Son most would comfort him least. Could it be that those whom God loves most are not shielded from suffering but given it? Suffering may not be the evil we thought it was, but a way for God to use us to redeem the world.

If you want to understand the relationship between a loving God and a suffering world, look to Jesus on the cross. There we see a loving God who dies for a suffering world so that the world might be made loving by God's suffering for it. One only has to read the Suffering Servant passage in Isaiah 52:13 – 53:12 to grasp the full impact of this truth, especially those hard words: "Yet it was the will of the Lord to crush him with pain" (Is. 53:10).

The Christian claim is that the life, death and resurrection of Jesus provide us with an understanding of suffering. We may never know why pain and suffering come our way, but we do have the resources to cope with it. Suffering united in Christ and borne in love is redemptive. St. Paul says, "I am now rejoicing in my sufferings for your sake, and in my flesh I am completing what is lacking in Christ's afflictions for the sake of his body, that is, the church" (Col. 1:24). Paul is saying that we can unite our sufferings to Christ and offer them for our good and the good of all people. Every pain we endure with love, every cross borne with resignation, benefits every person.

In another passage, St. Paul says: "And not only that, but we also boast in our sufferings, knowing that suffering produces endurance, and endurance produces character, and character produces hope, and hope does not disappoint us…" (Rom. 5:3-5a). A life without pain and suffering would be a life without healing and joy.

When pain comes our way, we are presented with choices. Do we try to deny it? Do we make it the center of our lives? Do we call it our enemy? Or do we consciously acknowledge our sufferings as a pathway to a deeper relationship with God? As countless faithful Christians have attested over the years, pain, while never welcome, can stretch us, cause us to grow spiritually, and help us see life in a new way. The noted author Flannery O'Connor called her lupus "more instructive than a long trip to Europe." That may not be true of everyone, but there is no doubt that suffering borne in faith can unite us to the cross of Christ who took our sufferings upon himself.

Suffering and Love

Suffering love is the way of God. Why then, is there so much loveless suffering? Here lies the mystery of fallen human nature. Life presents us with a choice between loveless suffering and suffering love. Choose we must. I don't know of any third option. When suffering comes our way, the issue is how we will cope with it.

Some people choose loveless suffering by choosing not to suffer at all. In Roman mythology, the temptation of Cupid is not only to have romance without sacrifice, but love without suffering. That is impossible. Love and your heart may be broken is a truism that all lovers know at some point in their lives. Do not the marriage vows remind us that we may have to suffer in our love for our spouse? Christian marriage, after all, is for better or worse; for richer or poorer; in sickness and in health. Marriage inevitably breaks down when we refuse to accept the suffering aspect of love. For then, we not only reject the possibility of authentic marriage, but we deny our existential condition as created beings.

The lure of Cupid always ends in pain because the effort to escape from suffering leads to more suffering. If we try to love without suffering, we will end up suffering without love. The pursuit of pleasure is not the possession of happiness. There are enough broken hearts and broken lives in the world that testify to the lie of Cupid.

Christ's words carry a solemn warning: "If any want to become my followers, let them deny themselves and take up their cross and follow me. For those who want to save their life will lose it, and those who lose their life for my sake will find it. For what will it profit them if they gain the whole world but forfeit their life? Or what will they give in return for their life?" (Mt. 16:24-26).

It was Pope John Paul I, who in his all too brief reign, remarked, "The cross without Christ is too heavy to carry." Christ's love – and the love we offer one another – can get us through the tough times of life. We can walk through life knowing that we can make our share of mistakes and still feel love, accepted, and forgiven. We can face the future with hope even when our present circumstances seem to lead only to a dead end. We may still lose our lives, but we live confidently that death is not the end of life, God is. In the power of God's love, life is triumphant over death.

In one of my Bibles, I have a picture of an icon of the twenty-one Egyptian Coptic Christian martyrs who were beheaded by ISIS in Libya in February 2015. These Egyptian Christians were laborers, not priests or monks. They were in Libya to find work, make some money, and then return to Egypt to support their families. All were given a chance to save their lives if they would renounce their Christian faith and convert to Islam. None of them chose to do so. Reports have it, that as they were kneeling before their executioners ready to be beheaded, they called out the name of Jesus again and again. "Jesus, Jesus, Jesus" – that was their last word before dying.

Jesus was in their hearts as well as on their lips, and they would not forsake him even if that meant their deaths. None of them wanted to die, but they trusted that because Jesus lives, so would they. The living Christ lived in them, and therefore even in death, they did not die. They took to heart the words of Jesus: "I am the resurrection and the life. Those who believe in me, even though they die, will live, and everyone who lives and believes in me will never die" (Jn. 11:25-26). Amazing as it may seem, even today in the twenty-first century, people live and die for Jesus because in some mystical way, he is in them and they in him.

Coping with Suffering

No matter what our situation or the support we receive, suffering eludes our ability to control it. After all, if we could perfectly control our suffering, then we would no longer suffer. What makes suffering so insidious is the feeling of helplessness. Suffering evades our grasp; we feel frustrated by its power to dominate us. Life feels chaotic and out of control. Christian philosopher Soren Kierkegaard wrote that suffering involves *angst* – a dread of the unknown, a fear at the possibility of the absolute nothingness of our existence. If there is nothing beyond the grave, then the encounter with the possibility of nothingness is sheer dread.

To deal with suffering effectively, we must let go of our lives and relinquish our autonomy. It is precisely in this relinquishment that redemptive suffering becomes possible. Where personal faith is nourished in reception of Holy Communion, where prayer and the spiritual disciplines are practiced, where friends act as a support, where we belong to a community of faith that supports us in our pain, then suffering is more likely to be borne in love than become loveless suffering.

There is no perfect formula for coping with suffering. Still, during my years of ministry, I have witnessed people who found amazing strength in extreme adversity. They are the overcomers, life's victors. And while they faced different crises and sufferings, there was a commonality in what made them victors. Based on their hard-won experience, I want to share six ways to confront adversity.

First, trust God. Does that sound simplistic? Actually, it is an enormous challenge to trust God when we are in pain and the world around us is in disarray. It requires profound faith and resolute courage to trust God in the face of things we cannot understand or accept. St. Thomas Aquinas taught: "To one who has faith, no explanation is necessary. To one without faith, no explanation is possible." In the end, reconciling a loving God with a suffering world requires faith – first to trust the person of God, then to trust the plan of God. We have to believe *in* God before we can trust God's ways.

St. Paul wrote: "We know that all things work together for good for those who love God, who are called according to his purpose" (Rom. 8:28). God has a purpose for our lives – and for our suffering. We are to cultivate patience and confidence that God will sustain us through whatever difficulties come our way. As our trust increases, so too does our confidence that God will be with us through the pains of life. Even in darkest night, there is the hope of dawn.

Too many of us would rather retain mastery of our lives than let go and trust God. Suffering, however, is an invitation to radical openness to God. We are invited to approach the heavenly throne just as we are: mortal, finite, frail, and vulnerable creatures in need of our Creator's healing grace. We are thereby able to hear the words of the Lord speaking to us: "My grace is sufficient for you, for power is made perfect in weakness" (2 Cor. 12:9). As we become receptive to that grace, we gain strength for the journey ahead.

When I served two small churches in upstate New York, I knew a dear couple, Ruth and Richard. They were happily married for over fifty years.

Then, just days away from open heart surgery, Richard suffered a massive heart attack. What followed were weeks of uncertainty with Richard battling for his life.

At first, Ruth felt she had to hold onto God's hand tightly to get through the ordeal. There were times, however, when she was so tired, drained and weary, that she felt she couldn't hold on any longer. And just at that point of exhaustion, a revelation came to her. She didn't need to worry about holding God's hand so tightly anymore because God was holding her hand. Even if she let go, God would never let go. It was that quiet assurance of God's presence that gave Ruth the strength to carry on and nurse Richard back to health.

To say in the midst of crisis, "God never let's go!" – that is what it means to trust God.

When I was in divinity school at a particularly difficult time in my own life, I read Harry Williams' autobiography, *Some Day I'll Find You*. Harry Williams, a British Anglican monk of the Community of the Resurrection, was an accomplished theologian and preacher. Yet, he suffered a nervous breakdown. His world was completely shattered and he was unable to perform the simplest tasks – even to walk across the room. Then he began to recuperate, to come out of the other side of this devastating experience.

Harry recalled an experience on a winter's day shortly after World War II. There was not much fuel and the buildings were very cold. A light snow had fallen, and Harry decided to go for a walk to get warm. He entered Regent's Park as the sun was beginning to set. The air was unusually still, and the park was very beautiful with a glowing afternoon sun and shrubs dusted with patches of snow. It should have been a glorious experience but Harry was not able to appreciate the moment because of his illness. His life was unraveling and he could not appreciate anything.

And yet, the experience wasn't lost. As he began to recuperate and to emerge from his depression, he remembered that day. Months and even years later, when he had recovered, he continued to recall that afternoon, the sun's radiant light on the snow in the park. It was for him one of those gentle proofs of the divine in our midst. It was a taste of God's presence, of the wonder and mystery of life. It spoke to Harry and it kept speaking through the long months of his psychological ordeal, and was speaking still when he recovered and he could see the patterns of his own life.

God works in that way. When we are in pain, God is there, even when we feel overwhelmed and distraught. That is the good news: God never forsakes us or abandons us – never.

Second, think of others. This goes against our natural tendency to focus on ourselves when we hurt. Pain has a way of making us look inward, focusing on no one but ourselves. We become preoccupied with how to relieve our pain. And yet, Christians are admonished to think of others. St. Paul writes: "Let each of you look not to your own interests, but to the interests of others" (Phil. 2:4). In Galatians Paul says: "Bear one another's burdens, and in this way you will fulfill the law of Christ" (Gal. 6:2).

The worst thing we can do when we experience suffering is to feel sorry for ourselves. We then foreclose the possibility of our suffering as redemptive. We become impatient and distrustful of God; we close in upon ourselves as we block out the rest of the world. The preoccupation with ourselves distorts reality. We perceive our suffering out of proportion to the sufferings of others. Our sufferings and consequent needs become the measure of all things. That tendency should be resisted.

Thinking of the needs of others, even as we suffer, allows us the opportunity to break out of the bondage of the self. By seeing our suffering in perspective, as part of the suffering in the world, we see it as God sees it in his loving purpose. Leo Tolstoy put it like this: "If you feel pain, you are alive. If you feel other peoples' pain, you are a human being."

A husband and wife were taking a Sunday afternoon drive in the country to enjoy the fall foliage. Suddenly, the husband steered the car to the side of the road, stopped, and complained to his wife of chest pains. Within minutes he was dead of a heart attack. His wife went into severe depression. She became morose, passive, and lethargic. She secluded herself in her home, rarely leaving except to buy groceries. Finally, a neighbor came by and persuaded her to volunteer at her church's soup kitchen which served a hearty meal to needy people six days a week. She got involved with the soup kitchen and eventually became an active member of *Bread for the World*, an organization dedicated to combatting world hunger.

In telling me her story, she said, "Gary, I used to feel sorry for myself that my husband died in his 60s. But we lived well; we had everything we could reasonably want, and we lacked for nothing. And yet, there are people in the developing world who never make it to their 60s. They die of malnutrition, disease and lack of clean water. That's the real tragedy in the world. I am now glad to be able to do something about it."

That woman did not allow her anger over her husband's death to have the last word in her life. She channeled her anger to serve others and help make a better world.

I see this again and again with people who have experienced adversity in their lives. Where I live in the Phoenix, Arizona region, there are three organizations dedicated to serving persons with intellectual and physical disabilities. All three were started because families did not think there were enough services to adequately meet the needs of their special needs child, and therefore resolved to do something about it. Today all three organizations are thriving, meeting the needs of hundreds of younger and older adults, and making the Phoenix region one of the most attractive areas in the United States for persons with intellectual and developmental disabilities. Hopeful, positive, life-giving ministries came from people in pain, serving not only their own children but many others as well.

We may never know the *why* of suffering, but we can combat it. Suffering should make us want to do good; the pain of others should bring forth compassion in us. The tragedies of life should motivate us to trust God, even in the face of things we cannot understand or much less accept. As the widow who became involved in *Bread for the World* recognized, the real question when suffering comes our way is not why bad things happen to good people, but how do we respond to tragedy, to the pain and suffering of other people around us? If we want suffering to bring out the best in us and not the worst, then respond to the pain of others. It is the one sure way of healing the pain within ourselves.

Third, be thankful. St. Paul exhorts us to give thanks in all circumstances (1 Thess. 5:18). I recognize that many of us may have trouble with this. Should we really be thankful for the death of a loved one, or a cancerous lung, or a child on drugs, or the loss of a job? How can we be thankful for what appears to be evil, or at least tragic?

The answer is not to thank God for our suffering but to thank God in spite of our suffering. You may, for example, grieve deeply for a deceased spouse or loved one, or even a child who died, but you can still be thankful that you had time with that person in this life. Thankfulness and grief can go together. You thank God for the person coming into your life even as you grieve that person's death.

Years ago my uncle Joe died of a heart attack. He had been complaining of chest pain but delayed going to the doctor. While making a sales call at a business, he suddenly collapsed and passed out. Someone took hold of him before he hit the ground. The manager immediately called emergency. The ambulance arrived within minutes to take him to the hospital. Sadly, the doctors were unable to resuscitate him.

When I saw my aunt at the funeral home, she told me that oddly enough, she felt thankful. My uncle and aunt had been married for over thirty years and were very much in love. It would be hard for her to cope without him, she admitted. And yet, she had met so many wonderful people in the last few days. The manager at the company where my uncle collapsed assured her that they made him comfortable and called emergency immediately. The emergency crew told her they did all they could to stabilize his condition. The medical team at the hospital worked feverishly trying to resuscitate him. "Gary," she said to me, "there were so many good people that tried to help my husband. I can only thank God for that."

Thankfulness may not take away our pain, but it can help us cope with it. Still, there are occasions when thankfulness overrides the pain completely.

In my first parish on the Gaspe Coast of Quebec, I knew a woman who had been battling cancer for three years. She radiated joy every time I saw her. She loved the mountains, the sea and her little house. She never let a day go by without thanking God for being alive, and then living that day to the fullest. One some days that meant preparing a meal of cod tongues and boiled potatoes for her husband; or working in the garden; or baking bread; or gazing at the northern lights; or resting quietly in her rocking chair listening to music.

I remember one conversation over tea. She told me that her pain was becoming more intense, but that she was grateful she had time to suffer because so many die of cancer so quickly. Then she said something quite remarkable. She said, "Even the pain tells me I'm alive."

Too often we think that you have to be in perfect health to be thankful. That is simply not true. Some of the most joyful, thankful people are ones who are going through physical and emotional problems you and I can only imagine. What keeps them going? I believe it is a sense of thankfulness for the gift of life. As a parishioner who could hardly walk said to me, "Every morning I give thanks that I am on the top side of the ground and not under it." That man lived a contented life even in his pain. He recognized the gift of life – a life that may not have been perfect but was still worth living.

Years ago there was a controversy about thalidomide babies in Germany. A drug was given to expectant mothers to deal with nausea during pregnancy. However, the drug produced severely disabled children. At the time of their birth, some questioned whether such children should have been born. Would it not have been more merciful, more compassionate to abort these children so that they would never have to endure their deformities in life? Or should the doctors and parents simply have left the newborn babies to die?

As the children grew older, many of them were asked if they were happy to be alive, disabled as they were. Not one of them expressed any regret at being born. They all exhibited a love for life, a joy at being alive – more love and more joy perhaps than many adults not disabled. There is a lesson here for all of us: If we are thankful for what appears to be even the most minimal life, then life is no longer minimal but precious.

When suffering comes your way, tell God "thank you" – not for your suffering but in spite of it. Be thankful that you are a forgiven sinner called into companionship with Jesus. Be thankful that you can take a leap of faith and find God's arms waiting to catch you. Be thankful that when you walk "through the valley of the shadow of death," you never walk alone. Be thankful for peace in the midst of turmoil, confirmation in the midst of confusion, and life in the very act of dying. This is thankfulness in the deepest and most profound sense: having the quiet assurance that nothing can separate you from the love of God (Rom. 8:28). Know that God loves you, and the anxieties and uncertainties of this world lose their power to destroy you. When you walk in the way of Christ, the sufferings of this life will one day give way to the joy of resurrection. Bach's Cantata

56 expresses this sentiment well: "I will carry my cross gladly. It comes from the loving hand of God."

Fourth, outlast despair. The heartbreaks and heartaches of life afflict us all: broken down washing machines, sick children, bad news from the doctor, bewildering schedules, financial disasters, shaken marriages, the death of a loved one, and job terminations. Despair is when you work for a company for twenty-two years, suffer a heart attack, and then get fired for being sick. And yes, that really happened to a person I know!

When tragedies strike and difficulties come, we naturally ask God to remove them. God does sometimes rescue us from the troubles that bring us to our knees, but many times God doesn't. Often the hard times just keep coming, and when they do, we need the courage to outlast despair.

One of the religious figures I admire is the late Roman Catholic Archbishop of Chicago, Cardinal Joseph Bernardine. He was a strong advocate for what he termed a consistent ethic of life – from womb to tomb, the born and unborn, as he put it. Social justice, the sanctity of life, care for the poor and marginalized, were all part of his concern.

Cardinal Bernardine was extremely popular and there were Catholics who hoped he might be a candidate for Pope one day. Then a young man publicly accused Cardinal Bernardine of sexual misconduct. The charges were ravaging and destructive, but as it turned out, they were completely untrue. The young man withdrew the allegations and admitted they were totally false.

Several months later, the young man was on his own deathbed, dying of a fatal illness. Cardinal Bernardine, pastor that he was, went to the young man's bedside, blessed him and prayed that he receive the eternal peace of God. The Cardinal refused to allow the extreme hurt and humiliation of the young man's charges to have the last word in his life. He overcame the pain and opted for love.

Or consider William Sloan Coffin who was the Senior Minister at Riverside Church in New York City. He preached an inspiring sermon just one week after the death of his son Alex who was killed in an auto crash. He told the congregation, "Alex beat me to the grave." Then, he added, "If… a lamp went out, it was because for him at least, the Dawn had come." There in the worst of moments was the hope of resurrection.

We may never understand why bad things happen as they do – whether it be a false accusation against us or the sudden death of a loved one. Still, at any moment of crisis, we face a choice. We can let our pain turn us into bitter people, or we can move beyond the pain to become better people. We can let the hard blows of life knock us out and drag us down. Or we can rely on the power of God to face the future with faith. We can grow cynical, admit defeat, curse life, and believe that nothing really matters. Or we can affirm that God's power is greater than our problems; that God's grace is sufficient for our every need; and that God's love leads to life.

Soon after our daughter Allison was born with Down syndrome, there was a wonderful movie on television called *Kids Like These*. It was about an average American family who had a child; only this child had Down syndrome. The hospital scene was a poignant one. When the parents are told that their baby has Down syndrome, there is the usual shock and grief. Then the suggestion is made that perhaps the parents may want to put their baby in an institution so that they can get on with their lives as normally as possible – as if the baby had never been born.

The parents in the film chose to keep their baby. My wife Heather and I know their struggle. When Allison was born, our doctor, who meant well, gave us a book on people with intellectual and developmental disabilities living in state-run institutions. When we read the book, our hearts sank. We didn't want our daughter to live that way. We knew that God had a plan for our daughter even if we didn't know what that plan was just yet. God had given us this incredible gift, and we weren't about to turn her away. We brought her home, and in January 1986, I baptized her on the Feast of the Baptism of Christ. After the baptism, I said to the congregation that although I didn't know any of the details of her life, I was sure that Allison would be a light to the world. And you know something? She is.

We have choices in life. We have to make decisions one way or another. What choices we make largely depend on whether we can muster the courage to outlast despair. This is not to minimize the pain of being human, but there is always a life-giving way for all of us – a way of abundance in which we live in the power of God's love. Believing God cares about us, that God holds us precious in his sight, and that God sustains us every moment of our lives is the only sure way to turn our burdens into blessings and outlast despair.

Fifth, focus on Jesus. I know pain in my own life, and no doubt you do, too. There is the ache of the human heart, the loneliness of so many, and the evil that human beings are capable of inflicting on one another. We all have our scars, many of them unseen but as real as any on our bodies.

In her book *The Fire of Your Life*, Maggie Ross recounts the story of Emma, a survivor of the Holocaust. Regularly, at 4:00 p.m. each day, she stood outside a New York City church and screamed insults at Jesus. Finally, the priest went outside and said to Emma, "Why don't you go inside and tell him?" She disappeared into the church. An hour went by, and the worried priest decided to look in on her. He found Emma, prostrate before the cross, absolutely still. Reaching down he touched her shoulder. She looked up with tears in her eyes and said quietly, "After all, he was a Jew, too."[1]

We may be able to relate to Emma's pain, even if we have not experienced anything so monstrous as the Holocaust. When the world no longer makes sense, when everything we hold dear dies before us, when the foundation of our lives collapses, we can easily feel abandoned or forsaken.

When I ponder Mark's account of the crucifixion of Jesus, and his cry from the cross, "My God, my God, why have you forsaken me?" (Mk. 15:34), I imagine Jesus hanging there, slowly suffocating, his life slipping away, his strength sapped, the nails ripping his flesh, his muscles aching sore, hurting and disfigured, and feeling utterly abandoned. Here Jesus honestly expresses the same feeling of abandonment that has afflicted so many of us. When we believe ourselves to be isolated, cut-off, and alone in our pain, remember that Jesus endured all that and more.

The crucifixion of Jesus is not a tale of God's indifference to human suffering, but God's identification with that suffering. Isaiah in his Suffering Servant passage declares, "Yet it was the will of the Lord to crush him with pain" (Is. 53:10). There is a mystery here: only by undergoing suffering could God redeem it. The crucified God hangs where not even human beings should have to come. God is there – in the worst places, in the worst situations, in the worst-case scenarios of our lives. God suffers with us and for us, and saves us when we cannot save ourselves from sin and death.

In 1986, Soviet firemen and other rescue workers gave their lives to put out the nuclear fire at Chernobyl. These workers entered the power plant knowing full well they would likely not come out alive. In recognition of their sacrifice, the Russian newspaper Pravda published this anonymous poem:

> *God is a man who walked into a radiated complex,*
> *Put out the fire, burned his skin and clothes,*
> *Who didn't save himself,*
> *But saved Odessa and Kiev,*
> *A man who simply acted like a human being.*

God was there in that nuclear inferno, revealed through men making the supreme sacrifice as they plunged into a fiery nightmare. God doesn't avoid the chaos, the pain and darkness of human life. Rather God enters into it, taking it upon himself to redeem it. When Jesus rose from the dead on that first Easter Sunday, he gave proof to all of us that suffering, anguish, adversity and disappointment need never have the last word in our lives. In Jesus we believe in a God of life, truth and love, and therefore even in the darkest days, the light still shines in our lives.

Jesus on the cross is an image of hope and not despair. Empowered by the crucified God, we affirm life because our Savior conquered death. We bear our suffering because God bore his. We carry our cross because Jesus carries it with us. In response to the mystery of undeserved suffering, Jesus brings us the gift of unmerited love. In gazing at Jesus hanging on the cross, the question is never "Jesus, what did you do to deserve this?" but, "What have we done to deserve you?" On the cross Jesus showed us the depths of his love, the innocent suffering for the guilty.

In times of suffering, pain and anguish, look to the cross and the man hanging on it. His suffering makes our suffering bearable. Gazing on him will lighten our burden, however heavy it may be. Focusing on Jesus will strengthen and sustain us, and not allow us to grow fainthearted and despondent. Although our suffering may seem irrational, unintelligible and indefensible, we can better bear it if we focus on Jesus.

Sixth, live your life as if God reigns. There are times when the best of us get discouraged by what is happening in the world or with our own lives. Life may appear so dim that we can hardly see the light. We may wonder: ""Where is God in a world like this?" Well, God is where God has always been – reigning as Lord of all. God is God even in the worst of circumstances.

In his enthronement sermon as Archbishop of Canterbury in 1942, with German bombs devastating London and Britain threatened with invasion, William Temple preached that no matter what happens to us in this life, God reigns. In triumphs and tragedies, in victories and defeats, in the worst of times and in the best of times, God reigns. We might add that in sickness and in health, in our joys and sorrows, in bull markets and bear markets, in our job acceptances and job rejections, in our exhilarations and disappointments, and in all the ups and downs of life, God reigns.

This is the victory of Easter. You can try to kill God, you can nail God to a cross, you can place God in a tomb, you can roll a stone in front of the entrance, but you can't keep God dead and buried. Jesus lives! God reigns!

We all have problems, to be sure. Life can be tough. Sometimes we may feel that it is impossible to get through life without a broken heart. Tragedy happens, but it does not have the last word, God does. Evil, injustice, cruelty, and oppression do not have the last word, God does. Pain and suffering, tears and grief do not have the last word, God does. Our God is stronger by far than all the powers of darkness. In Jesus God has won the victory. There are battles and skirmishes to be sure, but the victory is assured by the death and resurrection of Jesus.

There is a well-known story about the actor Charlton Heston working on the movie *Ben-Hur* which was directed by Cecil DeMille. Heston had to perform a scene in the all-important chariot race at the end of the movie. DeMille decided that Heston should actually learn how to drive a chariot rather than use a stunt double. Heston agreed to take chariot lessons to make the movie as authentic as possible.

Learning to drive a chariot with horses, four abreast, was no small matter. After extensive work and days of practice, Heston returned to the movie set and reported to DeMille. "I think I can drive the chariot all right, Cecil," said Heston, "but I am not at all sure I can actually win the race."

Smiling lightly, DeMille said, "Heston, you just stay in the race, and I'll make sure you win."

Those are the words God speaks to us when we suffer and get discouraged. "Just stay in the race, and I'll make sure you win." We may not be able to see God's hand at work in the world or in our lives. We may never understand why bad things happen to good people, or good things happen to bad people. We may see all the heartbreaks and heartaches in people and think that God is absent from what is happening. It may be that only when we look back on events that we see God's purpose.

I realized this truth when I was visiting the Cloisters in New York City. The Cloisters is a Spanish medieval monastery transported stone by stone to the upper end of Manhattan, to Washington Heights park. The complex contains magnificent medieval exhibits, including beautiful tapestries of brilliant colors and fine artistry. When you look at the back of these tapestries, there are all sorts of threads that make no sense whatsoever. Only when you look at the front do you see the magnificent designs, shapes and images. The back side is chaos; the front side is order.

The biblical testimony is that there is a pattern to all of life. Often, however, we cannot discern it any more than we can see the artistic beauty of a medieval tapestry by viewing its back side. However, if we could see the front side of the tapestry, we would see the pattern, and we would see that all things do work for the good of those who love God. We live between the uncertainty of what is and what will be. All we know now is that God's plan for the world and our lives will not be frustrated.

None of this is to minimize your own pain, whether it is battling sickness and infirmity, or grieving the loss of a loved one, or paying the bills for another month, or being unemployed, or simply suffering from a broken heart at the state of our world. I know people who are in deep distress that the church is in steep decline with no end in sight. There are all sorts of pains and problems in life, heartbreaks and heartaches a plenty, without any simple solutions.

And yet, as Archbishop William Temple preached, God reigns always and forever. Look to God's victory in Jesus to find the confidence to get through whatever life throws your way.

The Scottish author Robert Louis Stevenson, on one of his voyages to the South Seas, told about a terrific storm that frightened all the passengers. One man finally went on deck and watched the captain pace the bridge, calm and undisturbed. He came back to the cabin where the passengers were huddled together and said to them, "I have seen the captain's face, and all is well."

Keep that in mind when adversity comes your way. No matter what happens, God is sovereign. God doesn't cease to be God because one person has cancer, another has a heart attack, and a third goes bankrupt. No matter what happens, God is in control. Even in the worst case scenario for any of us, the plan and purpose of God will not be frustrated. Therefore, we are not to lose heart. We are to stand fast in the faith, knowing that at the end of history, the end of life, God triumphs and Christ wins.

Trust God. Think of others. Give thanks. Outlast despair. Focus on Jesus. Live your life as if God reigns. The plain truth is that Christ didn't just rise from the grave two thousand years ago. He is alive today; alive for you and me now, alive in all our struggles, doubts and disappointments; alive in all our joys and sorrows of being human. Even when we want to shut this God out of our lives – lock the door of our heart, bolt it and keep it sealed – this God always comes back, breaks-in even the most unlikely places and shines with a light that illumines even the most dreary circumstances.

Never lose heart, never give up on life, never give in to despair. Keep hope alive, hold fast to the truth, and persevere with courage and conviction that the victory of life has already been won in Jesus. Whatever your circumstances, shout "Alleluia!" Jesus is triumphant over this suffering world.

Questions

- What difference does Jesus make in how you understand and cope with suffering and adversity in your life?

- What do you think of the distinction between suffering love and loveless suffering? Do you think suffering and love sometimes go together? How so?

- As you reflect on the six ways of coping with suffering, is there one that stands out as most helpful to you?

Prayer: In all things may the most holy, the most just, and the most lovable will of God be done, praised, and exalted above all forever. Your will be done, O Lord, your will be done. The Lord has given, and the Lord has taken away; blessed be the name of the Lord now and always. – Anonymous

ENDNOTES

Lesson One

1 Jim Collins, *Good to Great*. Harper Business, 2001, 84-87.

Lesson Two

1 C.S. Lewis, *A Grief Observed*. HarperOne, 1961, 30.

Lesson Three

1 George Mannes, "How Should You Measure Success?" *Money*, October 2012, 100.
2 Clayton Christensen, James Allworth, Karen Dillon, *How Will You Measure Your Life?* Harper Collins, 2021, 2.

Lesson Four

1 Viktor E. Frankl, *Man's Search for Meaning*. Beacon Press, 2006, 115.
2 Ibid. 76
3 David Watson, *Fear No Evil*. Hodder Christian Paperbacks, 1990, 120.

Lesson Five

1 Elizabeth Kubler-Ross, *Death and Dying*. Scribner, 2014.
2 Thornton Wilder, *The Bridge of San Luis Rey and Other Novels 1926 – 1948*. The Library of America, 2009, 192.

Lesson Ten

1 Margaret Craven, *I Heard the Owl Call My Name*. Dell Publishing, 1973, 39.

Lesson Eleven

1. Robert Seymour Bridges and Joachim Neander, "All My Hope on God Is Founded." *The Hymnal 1982*. The Church Hymnal Corporation, 1986, 665.
2. C.S. Lewis, "The Efficacy of Prayer." *The World's Last Night*, HarperOne, 2017, 3. Lewis' essay, "The Efficacy of Prayer" originally appeared in *The Atlantic Monthly*, January 1959.
3. Ibid. 9-10.
4. Cardinal Terrence Cooke, "Pastoral Letter to the Archdiocese of New York." October 9, 1983.

Lesson 12

1. Anicius Boethius, *The Consolation of Philosophy*. Translated by Victor Watts, Penguin Classics, 1999, Book IV.
2. Bishop John Robinson, Farewell Letter dated June 8, 1983, reported in the *Church Times* (U.K.), June 1983.

Lesson 13

1. *Manual of Prayers*. Compiled by James D. Watkins, Pontifical North American College, 2011, 223.
2. Ibid. 237.
3. *Hearts on Fire: Praying with Jesuits*. Edited by Michael Harter, Loyola Press, 1993, 104.
4. Ibid., 117.
5. *Avery Dulles: Essential Writings from America Magazine* Edited by James T. Keane, Christian Classics, 2019, 292.
6. Georges Bernanos, *The Diary of a Country Priest*. Collins Fount Paperbacks, 1981, 253.

Pastoral Reflections

1. Maggie Ross, *The Fire of Your Life*. Seabury, 2007, July Holocaust.

FURTHER READING

Avery Dulles: Essential Writings from America Magazine. Edited by James T. Keane, Christian Classics, 2019.

Hearts on Fire: Praying with the Jesuits. Edited by Michael Harter, Loyola Press, 1993.

Manual of Prayers. Compiled by James D. Watkins, Pontifical North American College, 1995.

Manual for Suffering. Edited by Jeffrey Kirby, TAN Books, 2021.

The Book of Common Prayer according to the use of The Episcopal Church. Oxford University Press, 1990.

The Book of Common Prayer 1662, International Edition. IVP Academic, 2021.

The Prayers and Meditations of St. Anselm. Translated by Sister Benedicta Ward, Penguin Books, 1973.

Andersen, Francis, *Job: An Introduction and Commentary.* Tyndale Old Testament Commentaries Vol. 14. IVP Academic, 2008.

Atkinson, David J., *The Message of Job.* IVP Academic, 2022.

Beck, Martha, *Expecting Adam.* Three Rivers Press, 1999.

Bernanos, Georges, *The Diary of a Country Priest.* Collins Fount Paperback, 1981.

Boethius, Anicius, *The Consolation of Philosophy.* Translated by Victor Watts, Penguin Classics, 1999.

Bowler, Kate, *Everything Happens for a Reason: And Other Lies I've Loved.* Random House, 2019.

Brown, Michael, *Job: The Faith to Challenge God: A New Translation and Commentary.* Hendrickson Publishers, 2019.

Camus, Albert, *The Plague.* Vintage, 1991.

Christensen, Clayton, James Allworth, Karen Dillon, *How Will You Measure Your Life?* Harper Collins, 2012.

Collins, Jim, *Good to Great.* Harper Business, 2001.

Craven, Margaret, *I Heard the Owl Call My Name.* Dell Publishing Co., 1973.

Frankl, Viktor E., *Man's Search for Meaning.* Beacon Press, 2006.

Janzen, Gerald J., *Job: Interpretation: A Bible Commentary for Teaching and Preaching.* Westminster/John Knox, 2012.

Kennedy, Moorhead, *The Ayatollah in the Cathedral.* Hill and Wang, 1987.

Kubler-Ross, Elizabeth, *Death and Dying.* Scribner, 2014.

Kushner, Harold, *When Bad Things Happen to Good People.* Anchor, 2004.

Lewis, C.S., *A Grief Observed.* HarperOne, 2015.

_____, *The Problem of Pain.* HarperOne, 2017.

_____, *The World's Last Night and Other Essays.* HarperOne, 2017.

Nouwen, Henri, *The Wounded Healer.* Image Books, 1979.

O'Kelly, Eugene, *Chasing Daylight: How My Forthcoming Death Transformed My Life.* McGraw Hill, 2007.

O'Malley, William, *Redemptive Suffering: Understanding Suffering, Living with It, and Growing through It.* Crossroad, 1997.

Otto, Rudolph, *The Idea of the Holy.* Oxford University Press, 1958.

Ross, Maggie, *The Fire of Your Life.* Seabury, 2007.

Rubenstein, Richard L., *After Auschwitz: History, Theology and Contemporary Judaism.* Johns Hopkins Press, 1992.

Ruzicka, Diana, *Redemptive Suffering in the Life of the Church.* Diana L. Ruzicka Publisher, 2018.

Templeton, Charles, *Farewell to God: My Reasons for Rejecting the Christian Faith.* McClelland and Stewart, 1999.

Watson, David, *Fear No Evil.* Hodder Christian Paperbacks, 1990.

Wiesel, Elie, *Night.* Hill and Wang, 2006.

Wilder, Thornton, *The Bridge of San Luis Re and Other Novels 1926 – 1948.* The Library of America, 2009.

Yancey, Philip, *Where Is God When I Hurt?* Grand Rapids: Zondervan, 2002.

ABOUT THE AUTHOR

The Rev. Dr. Gary Nicolosi is an Episcopal priest, lawyer and author of *SOULFIRE: Preaching the Church's Message in a Secular, Postmodern World* and *A Concise History of the Book of Common Prayer*. He has pastored urban, suburban and rural churches, large and small, throughout the United States and Canada.

Gary is a retired but still active priest in the Episcopal Diocese of Arizona and a member of the Church Disciplinary Board. He has served as Interim Rector of Church of the Nativity, Scottsdale, Arizona, and presently serves as permanent supply priest at St. Alban's Episcopal Church, Wickenburg, Arizona.

In addition, Gary practices pro bono immigration and veterans law in Arizona, and is a member of the New York Bar, the American Bar Association and the Federal Bar Association. He is the founder of the Institute of Law and Religion, which focuses on the interaction of law, religion and morality in American culture.

Gary has degrees in philosophy from Fordham University (B.A.) and Georgetown University (M.A.). He received his Juris Doctor from Temple University Law School, his Master of Divinity from Trinity College, University of Toronto, and his Doctor of Ministry from Pittsburgh Theological Seminary. He lives in Peoria, Arizona with his wife Heather and daughter Allison.

BOOKS BY GARY NICOLOSI

SOULFIRE: Preaching the Church's Message in a Secular, Postmodern World

SOULFIRE spotlights today's secular, postmodern culture and unleashes a groundbreaking primer on preaching. Synthesizing a lifetime of experience, Gary shares his method of preaching and provides sermons organized around four critical areas: exploring faith, the spiritual journey, contemporary issues and church life. The sermons are for any Christians seeking to understand and communicate Christian faith in a way that touches hearts, engages minds and transforms lives in Jesus. Seekers and skeptics also will benefit from this book as they come to explore Christianity in a thoughtful, honest and heartfelt way.

A Concise History of the Book of Common Prayer: An Appreciation of Anglicanism

A Concise History of the Book of Common Prayer is suitable for church forums and private study. Each chapter includes questions to guide group discussion and to provide serious personal reflection. Clergy, laity and students of Anglican history and theology will find in this work a dramatic narrative and an invitation to deepen their faith. The book is commended by the Episcopal Booksellers Association.

Both books are available in paperback and electronic versions through Amazon, Barnes and Noble, Apple and Chapters Indigo.

Made in the USA
Las Vegas, NV
05 February 2023